The Soul of Prayer

by

P. T. Forsyth

2014 edition. Thinking Anew Media. Los Angeles, CA

Contents

Dedication

TO

MRS. WATERHOUSE

Lomberdale Hall, in the High Peak

There is, high among the hills, a garden with a walk--a terraced walk. The moors lie round it, and the heights face it; and below the village drowses; while far, far afield, the world agonizes in a solemn tragedy of righteousness (where you, too, have your sepulchres)--a tragedy not quite divorced from the war in heaven, nor all unworthy of the glorious cusp of sky that roofs the riot of the hills.

The walk begins with a conservatory of flowers and it ends in an old Gothic arch--rising, as it were, from beauty natural and frail to beauty spiritual and eternal. And it curves and twines between rocky plants, as if to suggest how arduous the passage from the natural to the spiritual is. And it has, half-way, a little hermitage on it, like a wayside chapel, of old carved and inscribed stones. And the music and the pictures! Close by, the mowers whir upon the lawn, and the thrust flutes in the birch hedge; beyond, in the gash of the valley, the stream purrs up through the steep woods; still farther, the limestone rocks rise fantastic, like castles in the air; and, over all, the lark still soars and sings in the sun (as he does even in Flanders), and makes melody in his heart to the Lord.

That terrace was made with a purpose and a welcome

at will. And it is good to pace the Italian paving, to tread the fragrance from the alyssum in the seams, to brood upon the horizons of the far, long wolds, with their thread of road rising and vanishing into busy Craven, and all the time to think greatly of God and kindly of men--faithfully of the past, lovingly of the present, and hopefully of the future.

So in our soul let us make a cornice road for God to come when He will, and walk upon our high places. And a little lodge and shelter let us have on it, of sacred stones, a shrine of ancient writ and churchly memories. Let us make an eyrie there of large vision and humane, a retreat of rest and refitting for a dreadful world. May He show us, up there apart, transfigured things in a noble light. May He prepare us for the sorrows of the valley by a glorious peace, and for the action of life by a fellowship gracious, warm, and noble (as even earthly friendships may be). So may we face all the harsh realisms of Time in the reality, power, and kindness of the Eternal, whose Mercy is as His Majesty for ever.

CHAPTER I

The Inwardness of Prayer

It is difficult and even formidable thing to write on prayer, and one fears to touch the Ark. Perhaps no one ought to undertake it unless he has spent more toil in the practice of prayer than on its principle. But perhaps also the effort to look into its principle may be graciously regarded by Him who ever liveth to make intercession as itself a prayer to know better how to pray. All progress in prayer is an answer to prayer--our own or another's. And all true prayer promotes its own progress and increases our power to pray.

The worst sin is prayerlessness. Overt sin, or crime, or the glaring inconsistencies which often surprise us in Christian people are the effect of this, or its punishment. We are left by God for lack of seeking Him. The history of the saints shows often that their lapses were the fruit and nemesis of slackness or neglect in prayer. Their life, at seasons, also tended to become inhuman by their spiritual solitude. They left men, and were left by men, because they did not in their contemplation find God; they found but the thought or the atmosphere of God. Only living prayer keeps loneliness humane. It is the great producer of sympathy. Trusting the God of Christ, and transacting with Him, we come into tune with men. Our egoism retires before the coming of God, and into the clearance there comes with our Father our brother. We realize man as he is in God and for God, his Lover. When God fills our heart He makes more room for man than the humanist heart can find. Prayer is an act, indeed *the* act, of fellowship. We cannot truly pray even for ourselves without passing beyond ourselves and our individual experience. If we should begin with these the nature of prayer carries us beyond them, both to God and to man. Even private prayer is common prayer--the more so, possibly, as it retires from being public prayer.

Not to want to pray, then, is the sin behind sin. And it ends in not being able to pray. That is its punishment-- spiritual dumbness, or at least aphasia, and starvation. We do not take our spiritual food, and so we falter, dwindle, and die. "In the sweat of your brow ye shall eat your bread." That has been said to be true both of physical and spiritual labour. It is true both of the life of bread and of the bread of life.

Prayer brings with it, as food does, a new sense of power and health. We are driven to it by hunger, and, having eaten, we are refreshed and strengthened for the battle which even our physical life involves. For heart and flesh cry out for the living God. God's gift is free; it is, therefore, a gift to our freedom, i.e. renewal to our moral strength, to what makes men of us. Without this gift always renewed, our very freedom can enslave us. The life of every organism is but the constant victory of a higher energy, constantly fed, over lower and more elementary forces. Prayer is the assimilation of a holy

God's moral strength.

We must work for this living. To feed the soul we must toil at prayer. And what a labour it is! "He prayed in an agony." We must pray even to tears if need be. Our cooperation with God is our receptivity; but it is an active, a laborious receptivity, an importunity that drains our strength away if it do not tap the sources of the Strength Eternal. We work, we slave, at receiving. To him that hath this laborious expectancy it shall be given. Prayer is the powerful appropriation of power, of divine power. It is therefore creative.

Prayer is not mere wishing. It is asking--with a will. Our will goes into it. It is energy. *Orare est laborare.* We turn to an active Giver; therefore we go into action. For we could not pray without knowing and meeting Him in kind. If God has a controversy with Israel, Israel must wrestle with God. Moreover, He is the Giver not only of the answer, but first of the prayer itself. His gift provokes ours. He beseeches us, which makes us beseech Him. And what we ask for chiefly is the power to ask more and to ask better. We pray for more prayer. The true "gift of prayer" is God's grace before it is our facility.

Thus prayer is, for us, paradoxically, both a gift and a conquest, a grace and a duty. But does that not mean, is it not a special case of the truth, that all duty is a gift, every call on us a blessing, and that the task we often find a burden is really a boon? When we look up from under it it is a load, but those who look down to it from God's side see it as a blessing. It is like great wings--they increase the weight but also the flight. If we have no duty to do God has shut Himself from us. To be denied duty is to be denied God. No cross no Christ. "When pain ends gain ends too."

We are so egoistically engrossed about God's giving of the answer that we forget His gift of the prayer itself. But it is not a question simply of willing to pray, but of accepting and using as God's will the gift and the power to pray. In every act of prayer we have already begun to do God's will, for which above all things we pray. The prayer within all prayer is "Thy will be done." And has that petition not a special significance here? "My prayer is Thy Will. Thou didst create it in me. It is Thine more than mine. Perfect Thine own will"--all that is the paraphrase, from this viewpoint, of "Hear my prayer." "The will to pray," we say, "is Thy will. Let that be done both in my petition and in Thy perfecting of it." The petition is half God's will. It is God's will inchoate. "Thy will" (in my prayer) "be done (in Thy answer). It is Thine both to will and to do. Thy will be done in heaven--in the answer, as it is done upon earth--in the asking."

Prayer has its great end when it lifts us to be more conscious and more sure of the gift than the need, of the grace than the sin. As petition rises out of need or sin, in our first prayer it comes first; but it may fall into a subordinate place when, at the end and height of our worship, we are filled with the fullness of God. "In that day ye shall ask Me nothing." Inward sorrow is fulfilled in the prayer of petition; inward joy in the prayer of thanksgiving. And this thought helps to deal with the question as to the hearing of prayer, and especially its answer. Or rather as to the place and kind of answer. We shall come one day to a heaven where we shall gratefully know that God's great refusals were sometimes the true answers to our truest prayer. Our soul is fulfilled if our petition is not.

When we begin to pray we may catch and surprise ourselves in a position like this. We feel to be facing God from a position of independence. If He start from His end we do from ours. We are His *vis-a-vis;* He is ours. He is an object so far as we are concerned; and we are the like to Him. Of course, He is an object of *worship.* We do not start on equal terms, march up to Him, as it were, and put our case. We do more than approach Him erect, with courteous self-respect shining through our poverty. We bow down to Him. We worship. But still it is a voluntary, an independent, submission and tribute, so to say. It is a reverence which we make an offer. We present something which is ours to give. If we ask Him to give we feel that we begin the giving in our worship. We are outside each other; and we call, and He graciously comes.

But this is not Christian idea, it is only a crude stage of it (if the New Testament is to guide us). We are there taught that only those things are perfected in God which He begins, that we seek only because He found, we beseech Him because He first besought us (2 Cor. v. 20). If our prayer reach or move Him it is because He first reached and moved us to pray. The prayer that reached and moved us to pray. The prayer that reached heaven began there, when Christ went forth. It began when God turned to beseech us in Christ--in the appealing Lamb slain before the foundation of the world. The Spirit went out with the power and function in it to return with our soul. Our prayer is the answer to God's. Herein is prayer, not that we prayed Him, but that He first prayed us, in giving His Son to be a propitiation for us. The heart of the Atonement is prayer--Christ's great self-offering to God in the Eternal Spirit. The whole rhythm of Christ's soul, so to say, was Godhead going out and returning on itself. And so God stirs and inspires all prayer which finds and moves Him. His love provokes our sacred forwardness. He does not compel us, but we cannot help it after that look, that tone, that turn of His. All say, "I am yours if you will"; and when we will it is prayer. Any final glory of human success or destiny rises from man being God's continual creation, and destined by Him for Him. So we pray because we were made for prayer, and God draws us out by breathing Himself in.

We feel this especially as prayer passes upwards into praise. When the mercy we besought comes home to us its movement is reversed in us, and it returns upon itself as thanksgiving. "Great blessings which we won with prayer are worn with thankfulness." Praise is the converted consecration of the egoism that may have moved our prayer. Prayer may spring from self-love, and be so far natural; for nature is all of the craving and taking kind. But praise is supernatural. It is of pure grace. And it is a sign that the prayer was more than natural at heart. Spare some leisure, therefore, from petition for thanksgiving. If the Spirit move conspicuously to praise, it shows that He also moved latently the prayer, and that within nature is that which is above it. "Prayer and thanks are like the double motion of the lungs; the air that is drawn in by prayer is breathed forth again by thanks."

Prayer is turning our will on God either in the way of resignation or of impetration. We yield to His Will or He to ours. Hence religion is above all things prayer, according as it is a religion of will and conscience, as it is an ethical religion. It is will and Will. To be religious is to pray. Bad prayer is false religion. Not to pray is to be irreligious. "The battle for religion is the battle for prayer; the theory of religion is the philosophy of prayer." In prayer we do not think out God; we draw Him out. Prayer is where our thought of God passes into action, and becomes more certain than thought. In all thought which is not mere dreaming or brooding there is an element of will; and in earnest (which is intelligent) prayer we give this element the upper hand. We do not simply spread our thought our before God, but we *offer* it to Him, turn it on Him, bring it to bear on Him, press it on Him. This is our great and first sacrifice, and it becomes pressure on God. We can offer

God nothing so great and effective as our obedient acceptance of the mind and purpose and work of Christ. It is not easy. It is harder than any idealism. But then it is very mighty. And it is a power that grows by exercise. At first it groans, at last it glides. And it comes to this, that, as there are thoughts that seem to think themselves in us, so there are prayers that pray themselves in us. And, as those are the best thoughts, these are the best prayers. For it is the Christ at prayer who lives in us, and we are conduits of the Eternal Intercession.

Prayer is often represented as the great means of the Christian life. But it is no mere means, it is the great end of that life. It is, of course, not untrue to call it a means. It is so, especially at first. But at last it is truer to say that we live the Christian life in order to pray than that we pray in order to live the Christian life. It is at least as true. Our prayer prepares for our work and sacrifice, but all our work and sacrifice still more prepare for prayer. And we are, perhaps, oftener wrong in our work, or even our sacrifice, than we are in our prayer--and that for want of its guidance. But to reach this height, to make of prayer our great end, and to order life always in view of such a solemnity, in this sense to pray without ceasing and without pedantry--it is a slow matter. We cannot move fast to such a fine product of piety and feeling. It is a growth in grace. And the whole history of the world shows that nothing grows so slowly as grace, nothing costs as much as free grace; a fact which drives us to all kinds of apologies to explain what seems the absence of God from His world, and especially from His world of souls. If God, to our grief, seems to us far absent from history, how does He view the distance, the absence, of history from Him?

A chief object of all prayer is to bring us to God. But we may attain His presence and come closer to Him by the way we ask Him for other things, concrete things or things of the Kingdom, than by direct prayer for union with Him. The prayer for deliverance from personal trouble or national calamity may bring us nearer Him than mere devout aspiration to be lost in Him. The poor woman's prayer to find her lost sovereign may mean more than the prayer of many a cloister. Such distress is often meant by God as the initial means and exercise to His constant end of reunion with Him. His patience is so long and kind that He is willing to begin with us when we are no farther on than to use Him as a means of escape or relief. The holy Father can turn to His own account at last even the exploiting egoism of youth. And He gives us some answer, though the relief does not come, if He keep us praying, and ever more instant and purified in prayer. Prayer is never rejected so long as we do not cease to pray. The chief failure of prayer is its cessation. Our importunity is a part of God's answer, both of His answer to us and ours to Him. He is sublimating our idea of prayer, and realizing the final purpose in all trouble of driving us farther in on Himself. A homely image has been used. The joiner, when he glues together two boards, keeps them tightly clamped till the cement sets, and the outward pressure is no more needed; then he unscrews. So with the calamities, depressions, and disappointments that crush us into close contact with God. The pressure on us is kept up till the soul's union with God is set. Instant relief would not establish the habit of prayer, though it might make us believe in it with a promptitude too shallow to last or to make it the principle of our soul's life at any depth. A faith which is based chiefly on impetration might become more of a faith in prayer than a faith in God. If we got all we asked for we should soon come to treat Him as a convenience, or the request as a magic. The reason of much bewilderment about prayer is that we are less occupied about faith in God than about faith in prayer. In a like way we are misled about the question of immortality because we become more occupied with the soul than with God, and with its endless duration more than its eternal life, asking if we shall be in eternity more than eternity in us.

In God's eyes the great object of prayer is the opening or restoring of free communion with Himself in a kingdom of Christ, a life communion which may even, amid our duty and service, become as unconscious as the beating of our heart. In this sense every true prayer brings its answer with it; and that not "reflexly" only, in our pacification of soul, but objectively in our obtaining a deeper and closer place in God and His purpose. If prayer is God's great gift, it is one inseparable from the giver; who, after all, is His own great gift, since revelation is His Self-donation. He is actively with us, therefore, as we pray, and we exert His will in praying. And, on the other hand, prayer makes us to realize how far from God we were, i.e. it makes us realize our worst trouble and repair it. The outer need kindles the sense of the inner, and we find that the complete answer to prayer is the Answerer, and the hungry soul comes to itself in the fullness of Christ.

Prayer is the highest use to which speech can be put. It is the highest meaning that can be put into words. Indeed, it breaks through language and escapes into action. We could never be told of what passed in Christ's mountain midnights. Words fail us in prayer oftener than anywhere else; and the Spirit must come in aid of our infirmity, set out our case to God, and give to us an unspoken freedom in prayer, the possession of our central soul, the reality of our inmost personality in organic contact with His. We are taken up from human speech to the region of the divine Word, where Word is deed. We are integrated into the divine consciousness, and into the dual soliloquy of Father and Son, which is the divine give and take that upholds the world. We discover how poor a use of words it is to work them into argument and pursue their dialectic consequences. There is a deeper movement of speech than that, and a more inward mystery, wherein the Word does not spread out to wisdom, nor broods in dream, but gathers to power and condenses to action. The Word becomes Flesh, Soul, Life, the active conquering kingdom of God. Prayer, as it is spoken, follows the principle of the Incarnation with its twofold movement, down and up.[2] It is spirit not in expression only, but in deed and victory. It is speech become not only movement, but moral action and achievement; it is word become work; as the Word from being Spirit became flesh, as Christ from prophet became priest, and then Holy Spirit. It is the principle of the Incarnation, only with the descending movement reversed. "Ye are gods." God became man in His Son's outgoing that man might become divine; and prayer is in the train of the Son's return to the Father, a function of the Ascension and Exaltation, in which (if we may not say man becomes God) we are made partakers of the divine nature, not ontologically, but practically, experimentally. It is the true response, and tribute, and trophy to Christ's humiliation. Man rises to be a co-worker with God in the highest sense. For it is only action, it is not by dream or rapture, far less in essence, that we enter communion with an active being--above all with the eternal Act of God in Christ that upholds the world. As such communion prayer is no mere rapport, no mere contact. It is the central act of the soul, organic with Christ's; it is that which brings it into tune with the whole universe as God's act, and answers the beating of its central heart. It is a part and function of the creative, preservative, and consummatory energy of the world.

What is true religion? It is not the religion which contains most truth in the theological sense of the word. It is not the religion most truly thought out, not that which most closely fits with thought. It is religion which comes to itself most powerfully in prayer. It is the religion in which the soul becomes very sure of God and itself in prayer. Prayer contains the very heart and height of truth, but especially in the Christian sense of truth--reality and action. In prayer the inmost truth of our personal being locks with the inmost reality of things, its energy finds a living Person acting as their unity and life, and we escape the illusions of sense, self, and the world. Prayer, indeed, is the great means for appropriating, out of the amalgam of illusion which means so much for our education, the pure gold of God as He wills, the Spirit as He works, and things as they are. It is the great school both of proficiency and of veracity of soul. (How few court and attain proficiency of soul!) It may often cast us down, for we are reduced by this contact to our true dimensions-- but to our great peace.

Prayer, true prayer, does not allow us to deceive ourselves. It relaxes the tension of our self-inflation. It produces a clearness of spiritual vision. Searching with a judgment that begins at the house of God, it ceases not to explore with His light our own soul. If the Lord is our health He may need to act on many men, or many moods, as a lowering medicine. At His coming our self-confidence is shaken. Our robust confidence, even in grace, is destroyed. The pillars of our house tremble, as if they were ivy-covered in a searching wind. Our lusty faith is refined, by what may be a painful process, into a subtler and more penetrating kind; and its outward effect is for the time impaired, though in the end it is increased. The effect of the prayer which admits God into the recesses of the soul is to destroy that spiritual density, not to say stupidity, which made our religion cheery or vigorous because it knew no better, and which was the condition of getting many obvious things done, and producing palpable effect on the order of the day. There are fervent prayers which, by making people feel good, may do no more than foster the delusion that natural vigour or robust religion, when flushed enough, can do the work of the kingdom of God. There is a certain egoist self-confidence which is increased by the more elementary forms of religion, which upholds us in much of our contact with men, and which even secures us an influence with them. But the influence is one of impression rather than permeation, it overbears rather than converts, and it inflames rather than inspires. This is a force which true and close prayer is very apt to undermine, because it saps our self-deception and its Pharisaism. The confidence was due to a lack of spiritual insight which serious prayer plentifully repairs. So by prayer we acquire our true selves. If my prayer is not answered, I am. If my petition is not fulfilled, my person, my soul, is; as the artist comes to himself and his happiness in the exercise of the talent he was made for, in spite of the delay and difficulty of turning his work to money. If the genius is happy who gets scope, the soul is blessed that truly comes to itself in prayer.

Blessed, yet not always happy. For by prayers we are set tasks sometimes which (at first, at least) may add to life's burden. Our eyes being opened, we see problems to which before we were blind, and we hear calls that no more let us alone. And I have said that we are shown ourselves at times in a way to dishearten us, and take effective dogmatism out of us. We lose effect on those people who take others at their own emphatic valuation, who do not try the spirits, and who have acquired no skill to discern the Lord in the apostle. True searching prayer is incompatible with spiritual dullness or self-complacency. And, therefore, such stupidity is not a mere defect, but a vice. It grew upon us because we did not court the searching light, nor haunt the vicinity of the great white Throne. We are chargeable with it because of our neglect of what cures it. Faith is a quickening spirit, it has insight; and religious density betrays its absence, being often the victim of the sermon instead of the alumnus of the gospel. It is not at all the effect of ignorance. Many ignorant people escape it by the exercise of themselves unto godliness; and they not only show wonderful spiritual acumen, but they turn it upon themselves; with a result, often, of great but vigilant humility, such axis apt to die out of an aggressive religion more eager to bring in a kingdom coming than to trust a Kingdom come. They are self-sufficient in a godly sort, and can even carry others, in a way which reveals the action of a power in them beyond all natural and unschooled force. We can feel in them the discipline of the Spirit. We can read much habitual prayer between their lines. They have risen far above religion. They are in the Spirit, and live in a long Lord's day. We know that they are not trying to serve Christ with the mere lustiness of natural religion, nor expecting do do the Spirit's work with the force of native temperament turned pious. There are, even amongst the religious, people of a shrewd density or numble dullness who judge heavenly things with an earthly mind. And, outside the religious, among those who are but interested in religion, there may be a certain gifted stupidity, a witty obtuseness; as among some writers who *sans gene* turn what they judge to be the spirit of the age upon the realities of Eternity, and believe that it dissolves them in spray. Whether we meet this type within the Church or without, we can mostly feel that it reveals the prayerless temper whatever the zeal or vivacity may be. Not to pray is not to discern--not to discern the things that really matter, and the powers that really rule. The mind may see acutely and clearly, but the personality perceives nothing subtle and mighty; and then it comforts and deludes itself by saying it is simple and not sophisticated; and it falls a victim to the Pharisaism of the plain man. The finer (and final) forces, being unfelt, are denied or decried. The eternal motives are misread, the spell of the Eternal disowned. The simplicity in due course becomes merely bald. And all because the natural powers are unschooled, unchastened, and unempowered by the energy of prayer; and yet they are turned, either, in one direction, to do Christian work, active but loveless, or, on the other, to discuss and renounce Christian truth. It is not always hard to tell among Christian men those whose thought is matured in prayer, whose theology there becomes a hymn, whose energy is disciplined there, whose work there becomes love poured out, as by many a Salvationist lass, and whose temper is there subdued to that illuminated humility in which a man truly finds his soul. "The secret of the Lord is with them that fear Him, and He will show them His covenant." The deeper we go into things the more do we enter a world where the mastery and the career is not to talent but to prayer.

In prayer we do not ask God to do things contrary to Nature. Rather here ascending Nature takes its true effect and arrives. For the God we invoke is the Lord and Destiny of the whole creation; and in our invocation of Him Nature ends on its own key-note. He created the world at the first with a final and constant reference to the new creation, whose native speech is prayer. The whole creation thus comes home and finds itself in our prayer; and when we ask from the God of the whole Creation we neither do not expect an arbitrary thing. We petition a God in whom all things are fundamentally working together for good to such a congenial cry. So far from crossing Nature, we give it tongue. We lift it to its divinest purpose, function, and glory. Nature excels itself in our prayer. The Creation takes its true effect in personality, which at once resists it, crowns it, and understands it; and personality takes true effect in God--in prayer. If there be a divine teleology in Nature at all, prayer is the telos. The world was made to worship God, for God's glory. And this purpose is the world's providence, the principle of creation. It is an end present all along the line and course of natural evolution; for we deal in prayer most closely with One to whom is no after nor before. We realize the simultaneity of Eternity.

When we are straitened in prayer we are yet not victims of Nature, we are yet free in the grace of God--as His own freedom was straitened in Christ's incarnation, not to say His dereliction, to the finishing of His task. It is hard, it is often impossible, for us to tell whether our hour of constriction or our hour of expansion contributes more to the divine purpose and its career. Both go to make real prayer. They are the systole and diastole of the world's heart. True prayer is the supreme function of the personality which is the world's supreme product. It is personality with this function that God seeks above all to rear--it is neither particular moods of its experience, nor influential relations of it with the world. The praying personality has an eternal value for God as an end in itself. This is the divine fullness of life's time and course, the one achievement that survives with more power in death than in life. The intercession of Christ in heaven is the continuity and consummation of His supreme work on earth. To share it is the meaning of praying in the Spirit. And it has more effect on history than civilization has. This is a hard saying, but a Christian can say no otherwise without in so far giving up his Christianity.

"There is a budding morrow in midnight." And every juncture, every relation, and every pressure of life has in it a germ of possibility and promise for our growth in God and grace; which germ to rear is the work of constant and progressive prayer. (For as a soul has a history, prayer has its progress.) This germ we do not always see, nor can we tend it as if we did. It is often hidden up under the earthly relations, and may there be lost--our soul is lost. (It can be lost even through love.) But also is may from there be saved--and we escape from the fowler's net. It's growth is often visible only to the Saviour whom we keep near by prayer, whose search we invoke, and for whose action we make room in prayer. Our certainty of Him is girt round with much uncertainty, about His working, about the steps of His process. But in prayer we become more and more sure that He is sure, and knows all things to His end. All along Christ is being darkly formed within us as we pray; and our converse with God goes on rising to become an element of the intercourse of the Father and the Son, whom we overhear, as it were, at converse in us. Yet this does not insulate us from our kind; for other people are then no more alien to us, but near in a Lord who is to them what He is to us. Private prayer may thus become more really common prayer that public prayer is.

And so also with the universe itself as we rise in Christ to prayer. Joined with its Redeemer, we are integrated into its universality. We are made members of its vast whole. We are not detained and cramped in a sectional world. We are not planted in the presence of an outside, alien universe, nor in the midst of a distraught, unreconciled universe, which speaks like a crowd, in many fragments and many voices, and drags us from one relation with it to another, with a Lo, here is Christ, or there. But it is a universe wholly vocal to us, really a universe, and vocal as a whole, one congenial and friendly, as it comes to us in its Christ and ours. It was waiting for us--for such a manifestation of the Son of God as prayer is. This world is not now a desert haunted by demons. And it is more than a vestibule to another; it is its prelude in the drama of all things. We know it in another knowledge now than its own. Nature can never be understood by natural knowledge. We know it as science never can--as a whole, and as reality. We know it as we are known of God--altogether, and not in pieces. Having nothing, and praying for everything, we possess all things. The faith that energizes in Christian prayer sets us at the centre of that whole of which Nature is the overture part. The steps of thought and its processes of law fade away.

They do not cease to act, but they retire from notice. We grasp the mobile organization of things deep at its constant and trusty heart. We receive the earnest of our salvation--Christ in us.

> There, where one centre reconciles all things,
> The world's profound heart beats.

We are planted there. And all the mediation of process becomes immediate in its eternal ground. As we are going there we feel already there. "They were willing to receive Him into the boat, and straightway the boat was at the land whither they were going." We grasp that eternal life to which all things work, which gives all the waxing organization its being and meaning--for a real organism only grows because it already is. That is the mark of a real life. And soul and person is the greatest organism of all. We apprehend our soul as it is apprehended of God and in God, the timeless God--with all its evolution, past or future, converted into a divine present. We are already all that we are to be. We possess our souls in the prayer which is real communion with God. We enter by faith upon that which to sight and history is but a far future reversion. When He comes to our prayer He brings with Him all that He purposes to make us. We are already the "brave creature" He means us to be. More than our desire is fulfilled--our soul is. In such hour or visitation we realize our soul or person at no one stage of it, but in its fullness, and in the context of its whole and final place in history, the world, and eternity. A phase which has no meaning in itself, yet carries, like the humble mother of a great genius, an eternal meaning in it. And we can seize that meaning in prayer; we can pierce to what we are at our true course and true destiny, i.e. what we are to God's grace. Laws and injunctions such as "Love your neighbour," even "Love your enemy," then become life principles, and they are law pressures no more. The yoke is easy. Where all is forgiven to seventy times seven there is no friction and no grief any more. We taste love and joy. All the pressure of life then goes to form the crystals of faith. It is God making up His jewels.

When we are in God's presence by prayer we are *right,* our will is morally right, we are doing His will. However unsure we may be about other acts and efforts to serve Him we know we are right in this. If we ask truly but ask amiss, it is not a sin, and He will in due course set us right in that respect. We are sure that prayer is according to His will, and that we are just where we ought to be. And that is a great matter for the rightness of our thought, and of the aims and desires proposed by out thoughts. It means much both as to their form and their passion. If we realize that prayer is the acme of our right relation to God, if we are sure that we are never so right with Him in anything we do as in prayer, then prayer must have the greatest effect and value for our life, both in its purpose and its fashion, in its spirit and its tenor. What puts us right morally, right with a Holy God (as prayer does), must have a great shaping power on every part and every juncture of life. And, of course, especially upon the spirit and tenor of our prayer itself, upon the form and complexion of our petition.

The effect of our awful War[3] will be very different on the prayerful and the prayerless. It will be a sifting judgment. It will turn to prayer those who did not pray, and increase the prayer of those who did. But some, whose belief in God grew up only in fair weather and not at the Cross, it will make more sceptical and prayerless than ever, and it will present them with a world more confused and more destitute of a God than before; which can only lead to renewed outbreaks of the same kind as soon as the nations regain strength. The prayerless spirit saps a people's moral strength because it blunts their thought and conviction of the Holy. It must be so if prayer is such a moral blessing and such a shaping power, if it pass, by its nature, from the vague volume and passion of devotion to formed petition and effort. Prayerlessness is an injustice and a damage to our own soul, and therefore to its history, both in what we do and what we think. The root of all deadly heresy is prayerlessness. Prayer finds our clue in a world otherwise without form and void. And it draws a magic circle round us over which the evil spirits may not pass. "Prayer," says Vinet, "is like the air of certain ocean isles, which is so pure that there vermin cannot live. We should surround ourselves with this atmosphere, as the diver shuts himself into his bell ere he descends into the deep."

If there must be in the Church a communion of belief, there must be there also a communion of prayer. For the communion of prayer is the very first form the communion of belief takes. It is in this direction that Church unity lies. It lies behind prayer, in something to which prayer gives effect, in that which is the source and soul of prayer--in our relation with God in Christ, in our new creation. Prayer for Church unity will not bring that unity; but that which stirs, and founds, and wings prayer will. And prayer is its chief exercise. The true Church is just as wide as the community of Christian prayer, i.e. of due response to the gospel of our reconcilement and communion with God. And it is a thing almost dreadful that Christians who pray to the same God, Christ, and Saviour should refuse to unite in prayer because of institutional differences.

A prayer is also a promise. Every true prayer carries with it a vow. If it do not, it is not in earnest. It is not of a piece with life. Can we pray in earnest if we do not in the act commit ourselves to do our best to bring about the answer? Can we escape some king of hypocrisy? This is especially so with intercession. What is the value of praying for the poor if all the rest of our time and interest is given only to becoming rich? Where is the honesty of praying for our country if in our most active hours we are chiefly occupied in making something out of it, if we are strange to all sacrifice for it? Prayer is one form of sacrifice, but if it is the only form it is vain oblation. If we pray for our child that he may have God's blessing, we are really promising that nothing shall be lacking on our part to be a divine blessing to him. And if we have no kind of religious relation to him (as plenty of Christian parents have none), our prayer is quite unreal, and its failure should not be a surprise. To pray for God's kingdom is also so engage ourselves to service and sacrifice for it. To begin our prayer with a petition for the hallowing of God's name and to have no real and prime place for holiness in our life or faith is not sincere. The prayer of the vindictive for forgiveness is mockery, like the prayer for daily bread from a wheat-cornerer. No such man could say the Lord's Prayer but to his judgment. What would happen to the Church if the Lord's Prayer became a test for membership as thoroughly as the Creeds have been? The Lord's Prayer is also a vow to the Lord. None but a Christian can pray it, or should. Great worship of God is also a great engagement of ourselves, a great committal of our action. To begin the day with prayer is but a formality unless it go on in prayer, unless for the rest of it we pray in deed what we began in word. One has said that while prayer is the day's best beginning it must not be like the handsome title-page of a worthless book.

"Thy will be done." Unless that were the spirit of all our prayer, how should we have courage to pray if we know ourselves at all, or if we have come to a time when we can have some retrospect on our prayers and their fate? Without this committal to the wisdom of God, prayer would be a very dangerous weapon in proportion as it was effective. No true God could promise us an answer to our every prayer. No Father of mankind could. The rain that saved my crop might ruin my neighbour's. It would paralyse prayer to be sure that it would prevail as it is offered, certainly and at once. We should be terrified at the power put into our foolish hands. Nothing would do more to cure us of a belief in our own wisdom than the granting of some of our eager prayers. And nothing could humiliate us more than to have God say when the fulfilment of our desire brought leanness to our souls. "Well, you have it." It is what He has said to many. But He said more, "My grace is sufficient for thee."

CHAPTER II

The Naturalness of Prayer

We touch the last reality directly in prayer. And we do this not by thought's natural research, yet by a quest not less laborious. Prayer is the atmosphere of revelation, in the strict and central sense of that word. It is the climate in which God's manifestation bursts open into inspiration. All the mediation of Nature and of things sinks here to the rear, and we are left with God in Christ as His own Mediator and His own Revealer. He is directly with us and in us. We transcend there two thousand years as if they were but one day. By His Spirit and His Spirit's creative miracle God becomes Himself our new nature, which is yet our own, our destined Nature; for we were made with His image for our "doom of greatness." It is no mere case of education or evolution drawing our our best. Prayer has a creative action in its answer. It does more than present us with our true, deep, latent selves. It lays hold on God, and God is not simply our magnified self. Our other self is, in prayer, our Creator still creating. Our Maker it is that is our Husband. He is Another. We feel, the more we are united with Him in true prayer, the deep, close difference, the intimate otherness in true love. Otherwise prayer becomes mere dreaming; it is spiritual extemporizing and not converse. The division runs not simply between us and Nature, but it parts us within our spiritual self, where union is most close. It is a spiritual distinction, like the distinction of Father and Son in heaven. But Nature itself, our natural selves, are involved in it; because Nature for the Christian is implicated in Redemption. It "arrives." It is read in a new script. The soul's conflict is found in a prelude in it. This may disturb our pagan joy. It may quench the consolations of Nature. The ancient world could take refuge in Nature as we cannot. It could escape there from conscience in a way impossible to us, because for us body runs up into soul, and Nature has become organic with spirit, an arena and even (in human nature) an experience of God's will. It groans to come to itself in the sons of God. Redemption is cosmic. We do not evade God's judgment there; and we put questions about His equity there which did not trouble the Greek. It we take the wings of the morning and dwell in the uttermost parts of the earth, God still besets us behind and before. We still feel the collision of past and future, of conduct and conscience. If we try to escape from His presence there, we fail; the winds are His messengers, the fires His ministers, wars and convulsions instruments of His purpose. He is always confronting us, judging us, saving us in a spiritual world, which Nature does not stifle, but only makes it more universal and impressive than our personal strife. In Nature our *vis-a-vis* is still the same power we meet as God in our soul.

The voice that rolls the stars along
Speaks all His promises.

Our own natural instincts turn our scourges, but also our blessings, according as they mock God or serve Him. So Nature becomes our chaperone for Christ, our tutor whose duty is daily to deliver us at Christ's door. It opens out into a Christ whose place and action are not historic only, but also cosmic. The cosmic place of Christ in the later epistles is not apostolic fantasy, extravagant speculation, nor groundless theosophy. It is the ripeness of practical faith, faith which by action comes to itself and to its own.

Especially is this pointed where faith has its most pointed action as prayer. If cosmic Nature runs up into man, man rises up into prayer; which thus fulfils Nature, brings its inner truth to pass, and crowns its bias to spirit. Prayer is seen to be the opening secret of creation, its destiny, that to which it all travails. It is the burthen of evolution. The earnest expectation of the creation waits, and all its onward thrust works, for the manifestation of the sons of God. Nature comes to itself in prayer. Prayer realizes and brings to a head the truth of Nature, which groans being burdened with the passion of its deliverance, its relief in prayer. *"Magna ars est conversari cum Deo."* "The art of prayer is Nature gone to heaven." We become in prayer Nature's true artists (if we may so say), the vehicles of its finest and inmost passion. And we are also its true priests, the organs of its inner commerce with God, where the Spirit immanent in the world meets the Spirit transcendent in obedient worship. The sum of things for ever speaking is heard in heaven to pray without ceasing. It is speaking not only to us but in us to God. Soliloquy here is dialogue. In our prayer God returns from His projection in Nature to speak with Himself. When we speak to God it is really the God who lives in us speaking through us to Himself. His Spirit returns to Him who gave it; and returns not void, but bearing our souls with Him. The dialogue of grace is really the monologue of the divine nature in self-communing love. In prayer, therefore, we do true and final justice to the world. We give Nature to itself. We make it say what it was charged to say. We make it find in thought and word its own soul. It comes to itself not in man but in the praying man, the man of Christian prayer. The Christian man at prayer is the secretary of Creation's praise. So prayer is the answer to Nature's quest, as God is the answer to prayer. It is the very nature of nature; which is thus miraculous or nothing at its core.

Here the friction vanishes, therefore, between prayer and natural law. Nature and all its plexus of law is not static, but dynamic. It is not interplay, but evolution. It has not only to move, but to arrive. Its great motive power is not a mere instinct, but a destiny. Its system is not a machine, but a procession. It is dramatic. It has a close. Its ruling power is not what it rises from, but what it moves to. Its impulse is its goal immanent. All its laws are overruled by the comprehensive law of its destination. It tends to prayer. The laws of Nature are not like iron. If they are fixed they are only fixed as the composition is fixed at H20 of the river which is so fluid and moving that I can use it at any time to bear me to its sea. They are fixed only in so far as makes reliable, and not fatal, to man's spirit. Their nature is constant, but their function is not stiff. What is fixed in the river is the constancy of its fluidity. "Still glides the stream, and shall for ever glide." The greatest law of Nature is thus its bias to God, its *nisus* to return to His rest. This comes to light chiefly in man's gravitation to Him, when His prodigal comes home to Him. The forwardest creation comes to itself in our passion for God and in our finding of Him in prayer. In prayer, therefore, we do not ask God to do things contrary to Nature, though our request may seem contrary to sections of it which we take for the whole. We ask Him to fulfil Nature's own prayer.

The atmosphere of prayer seems at first to be the direct contrary of all that goes with such words as practical or scientific. But what do we mean by practical at last but that which contributes to the end for which the world and mankind were made? The whole of history, as the practical life of the race, is working out the growth, the emancipation of the soul, the enrichment and fortifying of the human spirit. It is doing on the large scale what every active life is doing on the small--it is growing soul. There is no reality at last except soul, except personality. This alone has eternal meaning, power, and value, since this alone develops or hampers the eternal reality, the will of

God. The universe has its being and its truth for a personality, but for one at last which transcends individual limits. To begin with the natural plane, our egoism constructs there a little world with a definite teleology converging on self, one which would subdue everybody and everything to the tributary to our common sensible self. On a more spiritual (yet not on the divine) plane the race does the like with its colossal ego. It views and treats the universe as contributory to itself, to the corporate personality of the race. Nature is here for man, man perhaps for the superman. We are not here for the glory of God, but God is here for the aid and glory of man. But either way all things are there to work together for personality, and to run up into a free soul. Man's practical success is then what makes for the enhancement of this ego, small or great. But, on the Christian plane, man himself, as part of a creation, has a meaning and an end; but it is in God; he does not return on himself. God is his nisus and drift. God works in him; he is not just trying to get his own head out. But God is Love. All the higher science of Nature which is the milieu and the machinery that give the soul its bent to love, and turn it out its true self in love. All the practice and science of the world is there, therefore, to reveal and realize love and love's communion. It is all a stage, a scenery, a plot, for a denounement where beings mingle, and each is enriched by all and all by each. It all goes to the music of that love which binds all things together in the cosmic dance, and which makes each stage of each thing prophetic of its destined fullness only in a world so bound. So science itself is practical if prayer end and round all. It is the theory of a cosmic movement with prayer for its active end. And it is an ethical science at last, it is a theology, if the Christian end is the real end of the whole world. All knowledge serves love and love's communion. For Christian faith a universe is a universe of souls, an organism of persons, which is the expression of an Eternal Will of love. This love is the real presence which gives meaning, and movement, and permanence to a fleeting world of sense. And it is by prayer that we come into close and conscious union with this universe and power of love, this living reality of things. Prayer (however miraculous) is, therefore, the most natural things in the world. It is the effectuation of all Nature, which comes home to roost there, and settles to its rest. It is the last word of all science, giving it contact with a reality which, as science alone, it cannot reach. And it is also the most practical things in all man's action and history, as doing most to bring to pass the spiritual object for which all men and all things exist and strive.

Those who feel prayer stifled by the organization of law do not consider that law itself, if we take a long enough sweep, keeps passing us on to prayer. Law rises from Nature, through history, to heaven. It is integrated historically, i.e. by Christ's cross and the Church's history, with the organization of love. But that is the organization of Eternity in God, and it involves the interaction of all souls in a communion of ascending prayer. Prayer is the native movement of the spiritual life that receives its meaning and its soul only in Eternity, that works in the style and scale of Eternity, owns its principles, and speaks its speech. It is the will's congenial surrender to that Redemption and Reconciliation between loving wills which is God's Eternity acting in time. We beseech God because He first besought us.

So not to pray on principle means that thought has got the better of the will. The question is whether thought includes will or will thought; and thought wins if prayer is suppressed. Thought and not personality is then in command of the universe. If will is but a function of the idea, then prayer is but a symptom, it is not a power. It belongs to the phenomenology of the Infinite, it is not among its controls.

Prayer is doing God's will. It is letting Him pray in us. We look for answer because His fullness is completely equal to His own prayers. Father and Son are perfectly adequate to each other. That is the Holy Spirit and self-sufficiency of the Godhead.

If God's will is to be done on earth as it is in heaven, prayer begins with adoration. Of course, it is thanks and petition; but before we give even our prayer we must first receive. The Answerer provides the very prayer. What we do here rests on what God has done. What we offer is drawn from us by what He offers. Our self-oblation stands on His; and the spirit of prayer flows from the gift of the Holy Ghost, the great Intercessor. Hence praise and adoration of His work in itself comes before even our thanksgiving for blessings to us. At the height of prayer, if not at its beginning, we are preoccupied with the great and glorious thing God has done for His own holy name in Redemption, apart from its immediate and particular blessing to us. We are blind for the time to ourselves. We cover our faces with our wings and cry "Holy, holy, holy is the Lord God of hosts; the fullness of the earth is His glory." Our full hearts glorify. We magnify His name. His perfections take precedence of our occasions. We pray for victory in the present was, for instance, and for deliverance from all war, for the sake of God's kingdom-- in a spirit of adoration for the deliverance there that is not destroyed, or foiled, even by a devilry like this. If the kingdom of God not only got over the murder of Christ, but made it its great lever, there is nothing that it cannot get over, and nothing it cannot turn to eternal blessing and to the glory of the holy name. But to the perspective of this faith, and to its vision of values so alien to human standards, we can rise only in prayer.

But it would be unreal prayer which was adoration only, with no reference to special boons or human needs. That would be as if God recognized no life but His own-- which is very undivine egoism, and its collective form is the religion of mere nationalism. In true prayer we do two things. We go out of ourselves, being lost in wonder, love and praise; but also, and in the same act, we go in upon ourselves. We stir up all that is within us to bless and hallow God's name. We examine ourselves keenly in that patient light, and we find ourselves even when our sin finds us out. Our nothingness is not burned and branded into us as if we had above only the starry irony of heaven. Our heart comes again. Our will is braced and purified. We not only recall our needs, but we discover new ones, of a more and more intimate and spiritual kind. The more spiritual we grow, the more we rise out of the subconscious or the unconscious. We never realize ourselves as we do when we forget ourselves after this godly sort in prayer. Prayer is not falling back upon the abyss below the soul; even as the secret of the Incarnation is sought in vain in that non-moral zone. Prayer is not what might be called the increased drone or boom of an unspeakable Om. But we rise in it to more conscious and positive relation with God the Holy--the God not abysmal but revealed, in whose revelation the thoughts of many hearts are revealed also, and whose fullness makes need almost as fast as it satisfies it.

After adoration, therefore, prayer is thanksgiving and petition. When we thank God our experience "arrives". It finds what it came for. It fulfills the greatest end of experience. It comes to its true self, comes to its own, and has its perfect work. It breathes large, long, and free, *sublimi anbelitu.* The soul runs its true normal course back to God its Creator, who has stamped the destiny of this return upon it, and leaves it no peace till it finds its goal in Him. The gift we thank for becomes sacramental because it conveys chiefly the Giver, and is lost in Him and in His praise. It is He that chiefly comes in His saints and His boons. In real revelation we rise for above a mere interpretation of life, a mere explanation of events; we touch their Doer, the Life indeed, and we can dispense with interpretations, having Him. An occurrence thus becomes a revelation. It gives us God, in a sacrament. And where there is real revelation there is thanksgiving, there is eucharist; for God Himself is in the gift, and strikes His own music from the soul. If we think most of the gift, prayer may subtly increase our egoism. We praise for a gift to us. We are tempted to treat God as an asset, and to exploit him. But true prayer, thinking most of the Giver, quells the egoism and dissolves it in praise. What we received came for another end than just to gratify us. It came to carry God to us, and to lift us to Him and to the consent of His glory. The blessing in it transcends the enjoyment of it, and the Spirit of the outgoing God returns to Him not void, but bringing our souls as sheaves with Him.

So also with the petition in our prayer. It also is purified by adoration, praise, and thanksgiving. We know better what to pray for as we ought. We do not only bring to God desires that rise apart from Him, and that we present by an act of our own; but our desires, our will, as they are inspired are also formed in God's presence, as requests.

They get shape. In thanks we spread out before Him and offer Him our past and present, but in petition it is our future.

But has petition a true place in the highest and purest prayer? Is it not lost in adoration and gratitude? Does adoration move as inevitably to petition as petition rises to adoration? In reply we might ask whether the best gratitude and purest thanks are not for answered petitions. Is there not this double movement in all spiritual action which centres in the Incarnation, where man ascends as God comes down? Does not man enlarge in God as God particularizes upon men? But, putting that aside, is the subsidence of petition not due to a wrong idea of God; as if our only relation were dependence, as if, therefore, will-lessness before Him were the devout ideal--as if we but acknowledge Him and could not act on Him? Ritschl, for example, following Schleiermacher, says, "Love to God has no sphere of action outside love to our brother." If that were so, there would be no room for petition, but only for worship of God and service of man without intercession. The position is not unconnected with Ritschl's neglect of the Spirit and His intercession, or with his aversion to the Catholic type of piety. If suffering were the only occasion and promptuary of prayer, then resignation, and not petition, might be the true spirit of prayer. But our desires and wills do not rise out of our suffering only, nor out of our passivity and dependence, but also out of our duty and our place in life; and therefore our petition is as due to God and as proper as our life's calling. If we may not will nor love, no doubt petition, especially for others, is a mistake. Of course, also, our egoism, engrossed with our happiness influences our prayer too often and too much. But we can never overcome our self-will by will-lessness, nor our greed of happiness by apathy. Petitions that are less than pure can only be purified by petition. Prayer is the salvation of prayer. We pray for better prayer. We can rise above our egoism only as we have real dealing with the will of God in petitionary prayer which does change His detailed intentions toward us though not His great will of grace and Salvation.

The element of adoration has been missed from worship by many observers of our public prayer. And the defect goes with the individualism of the age just past. Adoration is a power the egoist and individualist loses. He loses also the power both of thanksgiving and of petition, and sinks, through silence before God, to His neglect. For our blessings are not egoistically meant, nor do they remain blessings if so taken. They contemplate more than ourselves, as indeed does our whole place and work in the gift of life. We must learn to thank God not only for the blessings of others, but for the power to convey to others gifts which make them happier than they make us--as the gifts of genius so often do. One Church should praise Him for the prosperity of other Churches, for that is to the good of the gospel. And, as for petition, how can a man or a

Church pray for their own needs to the omission of others? God's fundamental relation to us is one that embraces and blesses all. We are saved in a common salvation. The atmosphere of prayer is communion. Common prayer is the inevitable fruit of a gospel like Christ's.

Public prayer, therefore, should be in the main liturgical, with room for free prayer. The more it really is common prayer, and the more our relation with men extend and deepen (as prayer with and for men does extend them), the more we need forms which proceed from the common and corporate conscience of the Church. Even Christ did. As He rose to the height of His great world-work on the cross His prayer fell back on the liturgy of His people--on the Psalms. It is very hard for the ordinary minister to come home to the spiritual variety of a large congregation without those great forms which arose out of the deep soul of the Church before it spread into sectional boughs or individual twigs.

Common prayer is not necessarily public. To recite the Litany on a sick-bed is common prayer. Christ felt the danger of common prayer as public prayer (Matt. vi. 5,6). And this is specially so when the public prayer is "extempore." To keep that real calls for an amount of private prayer which perhaps is not for every one. "Extempore" prayers are apt to be private prayers in public, like the Pharisee's in the temple, with too much idiosynerasy for public use; or else they lose the spontaneity of private prayer, and turn as formal as a liturgy can be, though in another (and perhaps deadlier) way. The prayers of the same man inevitably fall more or less into the same forms and phrases. But private prayer may be more common in its note than public prayer should be private in its tone. Our private prayer should be common in spirit. We are doing in the act what many are doing. In the retired place we include in sympathy and intercession a world of other men which we exclude in fact. The world of men disappears from around us but not from within. We are not indifferent to its weal or woe in our seclusion. In the act of praying for ourselves we pray for others, for no temptation befalls us but what is common to man; and in praying for others we pray with them. We pray for their prays and the success of their prayers. It is an act of union. We can thus be united even with churches that refuse to pray or unite with us.

Moreover, it is common prayer, however solitary, that prevails most, as being most in tune with the great first goal of God's grace--the community. So this union in prayer gives to prayer an ethical note of great power and value. If we really pray with others, it must clear, and consolidate, and exalt our moral relations with them everywhere. Could we best the man with whom and for whom we really pray? There is a great democratic note in common prayer which is also true prayer. "Eloquence and ardour have not done so much for Christ's cause as the humble virtues, the united activity, and the patient prayers of thousands of faithful people whose names are quite unknown." And we are united thus not only to the living but to the long dead. "He who prays is nearer Christ than even the apostles were," certainly than the apostles before the Cross and Resurrection.

We have been warned by a man of genius that the bane of so much religion is that it clings to God with its weakness and not with its strength. This is very true of that supreme act of religion of which our critics know least--of the act of prayer. So many of us pray because we are driven by need rather than kindled by grace. Our prayer is a cry rather than a hymn. It is a quest rather than a tryst. it trembles more than it triumphs. It asks for strength rather than exerts it. How different was the prayer of Christ! All the divine power of the Eternal Son went to it. It was the supreme form taken by His Sonship in its experience and action. Nothing is more striking in Christ's life than His combination of selflessness and power. His consciousness of power was equal to anything, and egoism never entered Him. His prayer was accordingly. It was the exercise of His unique power rather than of His extreme need. It came from His uplifting and not His despair. It was less His duty than His joy. It was more full of God's gift of grace than of man's poverty of faith, of a holy love than of a seeking heart. In His prayer He poured out neither His wish nor His longing merely, but His will. And He knew He was heard always. He knew it with such power and certainty that He could distribute His value, bless with His overflow, and promise His disciples they would be heard in His name. It was by His prayer that He countered and foiled the godless power in the world, the kingdom of the devil. "Satan hath desired to have thee--but I have prayer for thee." His prayer means so much for the weak because it arose out of this strength and its exercise. It was chiefly in His prayer that He was the Messiah, and the Revealer and Wielder of the power and kingship of God. His power with God was so great that it made His disciples feel it could only be the power of God; He prayer in the Eternal Spirit whereby He offered Himself to God. And it was so great because it was spent on God alone. So true is it that the kingdom of God comes not with observation, that the greatest things Christ did for it were done in the night and not in the day; His prayers meant more than His miracles. And His great triumph was when there were none to see, as they all forsook Him and fled. He was mightest in His action for men not when He was acting on men but on God. He felt the dangers of the publicity where His work lay, and He knew that they were only to be met in secrecy. He did most for His public in entire solitude; there He put forth all His power. His nights were not always the rest of weakness from the day before, but often the storing of strength for the day to come. Prayer (if we let Christ teach us of it) is mightiest in the mightiest. It is the ether round the throne of the Most High. Its power answers to the omnipotence of grace. And those who feel they owe everything to God's grace need have no difficulty about the range of prayer. They may pray for everything.

A word, as I close this chapter, to the sufferers. We pray for the removal of pain, pray passionately, and then with exhaustion, sick from hope deferred and prayer's failure. But there is a higher prayer than that. It is a greater thing to pray for pain's conversion than for its removal. It is more of grace to pray that God would make a sacrament of it. The sacrament of pain! That we partake not simply, nor perhaps chiefly, when we say, or try to say, with resignation, "Thy will be done." It is not always easy for the sufferer, if he remain clear-eyed to see that it is God's will. It may have been caused by an evil mind, or a light fool, or some stupid greed. But, now it is there, a certain treatment of it is God's will; and that is to capture and exploit it for Him. It is to make it serve the soul and glorify God. It is to consecrate its elements and make it sacramental. It is to convert it into prayer.

God has blessed pain even in causing us to pray for relief from it, or profit. Whatever drives us to Him, and even nearer Him, has a blessing in it. And, if we are to go higher still, it is to turn pain to praise, to thank Him in the fires, to review life and use some of the energy we spend in worrying upon recalling and tracing His goodness, patience, and mercy. If much open up to us in such a review we may be sure there is much more we do not know, and perhaps never may. God is the greatest of all who do good by stealth and do not crave for every benefit to be acknowledged. Or we may see how our pain becomes a blessing to others. And we turn the spirit of heaviness to the garment of praise. We may stop grousing and get our soul into its Sunday clothes. The sacrament of pain becomes then a true Eucharist and giving of thanks.

And if there were a higher stage than all it would be Adoration--when we do not think of favours or mercies to us or ours at all, but of the perfection and glory of the Lord. We feel to His Holy Name what the true artist feels towards an unspeakable beauty. As Wordsworth says:
I gazed and gazed,
And did not wish her mine.

There was a girl of 15, tall, sweet, distinguished beyond her years. And this is how Heine ran into English at the sight of her:
No flower is half so lovely,
So dear, and fair, and kind.
A boundless tide of tenderness
Flows over my heart and mind.

And I pray. (There is no answer
To beauty unearthly but prayer.)
God answered my prayer, and keep you
So dear, and fine, and fair.

CHAPTER III

The Moral Reactions of Prayer

All religion is founded on prayer, and in prayer it has its test and measure. To be religious is to pray, to be irreligious is to be incapable of prayer. The theory of religion is really the philosophy of prayer; and the best theology is compressed prayer. The true theology is warm, and it steams upward into prayer. Prayer is access to whatever we deem God, and if there is no such access there is no religion; for it is not religion to resign ourselves to be crushed by a brute power so that we can no more remonstrate than resist. It is in prayer that our real idea of God appears, and in prayer that our real relation to God shows itself. On the first levels of our religion we go to our God for help and boon in the junctures of our natural life; but, as we rise to supernatural religion, gifts becomes less to us than the Giver; they are not such as feed our egoism. We forget ourselves in a godly sort; and what we court and what we receive in our prayer is not simply a boon but communion--or if a boon, it is the boon which Christians call the Holy Spirit, and which means, above all else, communion with God. But lest communion subside into mere meditation it must concentrate in prayer. We must keep acquiring by such effort the grace so freely given. There is truly a subconscious communion, and a godliness that forgets God well, in the hourly life of taxing action and duty; but it must rise to seasons of colloquy, when our action is wholly with the Father, and the business even of His kingdom turns into heart converse, where the yoke is easy and the burden light. Duty is then absorbed in love--the deep, active union of souls outwardly distinct. Their connection is not external and (as we might say) inorganic; it is inward, organic, and reciprocal. There is not only action but interplay, not only need and gift but trust and love. The boon is the Giver Himself, and its answer is the self of the receiver. *Cor ad cor loquitor.* All the asking and having goes on in a warm atmosphere, where soul passes into soul without fusion, person is lost in person without losing personality, and thought about prayer becomes thought in prayer. The greatest, deepest, truest thought of God is generated in prayer, where right thought has its essential condition in a right will. The state and act of true prayer contains the very substance and summit of Christian truth, which is always there in solution, and becomes increasingly explicit and conscious. To grow in grace is to become more understanding in prayer. We make for the core of Christian reality and the source of Christian power.

Our atonement with God is the pregnant be-all and end-all of Christian peace and life; and what is that atonement but the head and front of the Saviour's perpetual intercession, of the outpouring of His sin-laden soul unto death? Unto death! That is to say, it is its outpouring utterly. So that His entire self-emptying and His perfect and prevailing prayer is one. In this intercession our best prayer, broken, soiled, and feeble as it is, is caught up and made prayer indeed and power with God. This intercession prays for our very prayer, and atones for the sin in it. This is praying in the Holy Ghost, which is not necessarily a matter either of intensity or elation. This is praying "for Christ's sake." If it be true that the whole Trinity is in the gospel of our salvation, it is also true that all theology lies hidden in the prayer which is our chief answer to the gospel. And the bane of so much theology, old and new, is that it has been denuded of prayer and prepared in a vacuum.

Prayer draws on our whole personality; and not only so, but on the whole God. And it draws on a God who really comes home nowhere else. God is here, not as a mere presence as He is in Nature, nor is He a mere pressure as He closes in upon us in the sobering of life. We do not face Him in mere meditation, nor do we cultivate Him as life's most valuable asset. But He is here as our Lover, our Seeker, our Visitant, our Interlocutor; He is our Saviour, our Truth, our Power, nay, our Spiritual World. In this supreme exercise of our personality He is at once our Respondent and our Spiritual Universe. Nothing but the experience of prayer can solve paradoxes like these. On every other level they are absurd. But here deep answers deep. God becomes the living truth of our most memorable and shaping experience, not its object only but its essence. He who speaks to us also hears in us, because He opens our inward ear (Rom. viii. 15; Gal.

<u>iv. 6</u>). And yet He is Another, who so fully lives in us as to give us but the more fully to ourselves. So that our prayer is a soliloquy with God, a monologue *a deux*.

There is no such engine for the growth and command of the moral soul, single, or social, as prayer. Here, above all, he who will do shall know. It is the great organ of Christian knowledge and growth. It plants us at the very centre of our own personality, which gives the soul the true perspective of itself; it sets us also at the very centre of the world in God, which gives us the true hierarchy of things. Nothing, therefore, develops such "inwardness" and yet such self-knowledge and self-control. Private prayer, when it is made a serious business, when it is formed prayer, when we pray audibly in our chamber, or when we write our prayers, guided always by the day's record, the passion of piety, and above all the truths of Scripture, is worth more for our true and grave and individual spirituality than gatherings of greater unction may be. Bible searching and searching prayer go hand in hand. What we receive from God in the Book's message we return to Him with interest in prayer. Nothing puts us in living contact with God but prayer, however facile our mere religion may be. And therefore nothing does so much for our originality, so much to make us our own true selves, to stir up all that is in us to be, and hallow all we are. In life it is not hard work; it is faculty, insight, gift, talent, genius. And what genius does in the natural world prayer does in the spiritual. Nothing can give us so much power and vision. It opens a fountain perpetual and huminous at the centre of our personality, where we are sustained because we are created anew and not simply refreshed. For here the springs of life continually rise. And here also the eye discerns a new world because it has second sight. It sees two worlds at once. Hence, the paradoxes I spoke of. Here we learn to read the work of Christ which commands the world unseen. And we learn to read even the strategy of Providence in the affairs of the world. To pray to the Doer must help us to understand what is done. Prayer, as our greatest work, breeds in us the flair for the greatest work of God, the instinct of His kingdom and the sense of His track in Time.

Here, too, we acquire that spiritual veracity which we so constantly tend to lose; because we are in contact with the living and eternal reality. Our very love is preserved from dissimulation, which is a great danger when we love men and court their love. Prayer is a greater school and discipline of divine love than the service of man is. But not if it is cut off from it.

And no less also is it the school of repentance, which so easily can grow morbid. We are taught to be not only true to reality, but sincere with ourselves. We cannot touch God thus without having a light no less searching than saving shed upon our own hearts; and we are thus protected from Pharisaism in our judgment of either self or friend or foe--especially at present of our foe. No companion of God can war in His name against man without much self-searching and self-humiliation, however reserved. But here humility turns into moral strength.

Here we are also regathered in soul from the fancies that bewilder us and the distractions that dissolve us into the dust of the world. We are collected into peace and power and sound judgment, and we have a heart for any fate, because we rest in the Lord whose judgments are salvation. What gives us our true stay gives us our true self; and it protects us from the elations and despairs which alternate in ourselves by bringing home to us a Saviour who is more to us than we are to ourselves. We become patient with ourselves because we realize the patience of God. We get rid of illusions about ourselves and the world because our intimacy is with the real God, and we know that we truly are just what we are before Him. We thus have a great peace, because in prayer, as the crowning act of faith, we lay hold of the grace of God the Saviour. Prayer alone prevents our receiving God's grace in vain. Which means that it establishes the soul of a man or a people, creates the moral personality day by day, spreads outward the new heart through society, and goes to make a new ethos in mankind. We come out with a courage and a humanity we had not when we went in, even though our old earth remove, and our familiar hills are cast into the depth of the sea. The true Church is thus co-extensive with the community of true prayer.

It is another paradox that combines the vast power of prayer both on the lone soul and on the moral life, personal and social, with the soul's shyness and aloofness in prayer. Kant (whose genius in this respect reflected his race) has had an influence upon scientific thought and its efficiency far greater than upon religion, though he is well named the philosopher of Protestantism. He represent (again like his race) intellectual power and a certain stiff moral insight, but not spiritual atmosphere, delicacy, or flexibility, which is rather the Catholic tradition. Intellectualism always tends to more force than finish, and always starves or perverts ethic. And nowhere in Kant's work does this limitation find such expression as in his treatment of prayer, unless it be in his lack of any misgivings about treating it at all with his equipment or the equipment of his age. Even his successors know better now--just as we in England have learned to find in Milton powers and harmonies hidden from the too great sagacity of Dr. Johnson or his time. Kant, then, speaks of prayer thus. If we found a man (he says) given to talking to himself we should begin to suspect him of some tendency to mental aberration. Yet the personality of such a man is a very real thing. It is a thing we can be more sure of than we can of the personality of God, who, if He is more than a conclusion for intellectual thought, is not more than a postulate for moral. No doubt in time of crisis it is an instinct to pray which even cultivated people do not, and need not, lose. But if any such person were surprised even in the attitude of private prayer, to say nothing of its exercise, he would be ashamed. He would think he had been discovered doing something unworthy of his intelligence, and would feel about it as educated people do when found out to be yielding to a superstition about the number thirteen.

A thinker of more sympathy and delicacy would have spoken less bluntly. Practical experience would have taught him discrimination. He would have realized the difference between shame and shyness, between confusion at an unworthy thing and confusion at a thing too fine and sacred for exposure. And had his age allowed him to have more knowledge and taste in history, and especially the history of religion, he would have gone, not to the cowardice of the ordinary cultivated man, but to the power and thoroughness of the great saints or captains of the race--to Paul, to Thomas a Kempis, to Cromwell with his troops, or Gustavus Adolphus with his. I do but humbly allude to Gethsemane. But Kant belonged to a time which had not realized, as even our science does now, the final power of the subtler forces, and the overwhelming effect in the long run of the impalpable and elusive influences of life. Much might be written about the effect of prayer on the great history of the world.

The Timeliness of Prayer

Let him pray now that never prayed before,
And him that prayed before but pray the more.

The nearer we are driven to the God of Christ, the more
we are forced on paradox when we begin to speak. I have
been led to allude to this more than once. The *magnalia
dei* are not those great simplicities of life on which some
orders of genius lay a touch so tender and sure; but they
are the great reconciliations in which life's tragic collisions
come to lie "quiet, happy and supprest." Such are the
peaceful paradoxes (the paradox at last of grace and
nature in the Cross) which make the world of prayer such
a strange and difficult land to the lucid and rational
interpreters of life. It is as miraculous as it is real that the
holy and the guilty should live together in such habitual
communion as the life of prayer. And it is another paradox
that combines the vast power of prayer for the active soul,
whether single or social, with the same soul's shyness
and aloofness in prayer.

There is a tendency to lose the true balance and
adjustment here. When all goes well we are apt to overdo
the aloofness that goes with spiritual engagement, and so
to sacrifice some of its power and blessing for the soul.
Prayer which becomes too private may become too
remote, and is apt to become weak. (Just as when it is
too intimate it becomes really unworthy, and may become
absurd even to spiritual men; it does so in the trivialities
associated sometimes with the answer to prayer.) It is

neither seemly nor healthy to be nothing but shy about the greatest powers in life. If we felt them as we should, and if we had their true vitality in us, we could not be so reserved about them. Some churches suffer much from extempore prayer, but perhaps those suffer more that exclude it. It at least gives a public consecration to prayer private and personal, which prayer, from the nature of it, must be extempore and "occasional." The bane of extempore prayer is that it is confused with prayer unprepared; and the greatest preparation for prayer is to pray. The leader of prayer should be a man of prayer--so long as prayer does not become for him a luxury which really unfits him for liturgy, and private devotion does not indispose him for public worship. Delicacy and propriety in prayer are too dearly bought if they are there at the cost of its ruling power in life, private and public, and of its prevailing power with God.

It is one of the uses of our present dreadful adversity⁴ that we are driven to bring the great two-handed engine of prayer frankly to the fore. There is probably a greater volume of personal prayer to-day than for generations we have had in this somewhat silent people, and there is less embarrassment in owning it. One hears tales of the humour in the trenches, but not so much of the prayer which appears, from accounts, to be at least equally and visibly there. And it is not the prayer of fear, either at home or abroad, but of seriousness, of a new moral exaltation, or at least deepening, a new sense of realities which are clouded by the sunshine of normal life. How can we but pray when we send, or our hearts go out to those who send, the dearest to the noble peril, or lose them in a noble death; or when we melt to those who are cast into unspeakable anxiety by the indirect effects of such a war upon mind or estate? We are helpless then unless we can pray. Or how can we but pray as we regain, under the very hand and pressure of God, the sense of judgment which was slipping from our easy and amiable creed? Above the aircraft we hear the wings of the judgment angel; their wind is on our faces; how should we not pray? We now discuss with each other our prayers as we have seldom done before; and we do it for our practical guidance, and not merely our theological satisfaction. We ask our neighbours' judgment if we may pray for victory when we can be so little sure as we are in the increased complexity of modern issues that all the right is on one side; or when our enemy is a great nation to which the Christianity and the culture of the world owe an unspeakable debt, whether for reformation or illumination. And if Christian faith and prayer is a supernatural, and therefore an international rivalries and tutelary gods?

Truly the course of events has been the answer to this question easier than at first. We are driven by events to believe that a great moral blindness has befallen Germany; that its God, ceasing to be Christian, has become but Semitic; that it has lost the sense of the great imponderables; that the idolatry of the State has barrack-bound the conscience of the Church and stilled that witness of the kingdom of God which beards kings and even beheads them. We are forced to think that the cause of righteousness has passed from its hands with the passing from them of humanity, with the submersion of the idea of God's kingdom in nationality or the cult of race, with the worship of force, mammon, fright, and ruthlessness, with the growth of national cynicism in moral things, and with the culture of a withering, self-searing hate which is the nemesis of mortal sin, and which even God cannot use as He can use anger, but must surely judge. This people has sinned against its own soul, and abjured the kingdom of God. That settles our prayer for victory. We must pray for the side more valuable for the kingdom of God--much as we have to confess.

It would more than repay much calamity if we were moved and enlarged to a surer sense, a greater use, and a franker confession of the power of prayer for life, character, and history. There is plenty of discussion of the present situation, historic, ethical, or political, and much of it is competent, and even deep. There is much speculation about the situation after the War, at home and abroad. But its greatest result may be the discredit of elegant, paltering, and feeble types of religion, the end of the irreligious wits and fribbles, and the rise of a new moral seriousness and a new spiritual realism. Many will be moved, in what seems the failure of civilization, to a new reliance on the Church, and especially on the more historic, ethical, and positive Churches, which have survived the paganism of culture and which ride the waves of storm. Yet even these impressions can evaporate unless they are fixed by action. And the action that fixes them in their own kind is prayer--prayer which is really action. A religion of prosperity grows dainty, petty, sentimental, and but pseudo-heroic. We unlearn our fathers' creed that religion is, above all things, an act, that worship is the greatest act of which man is capable, and that true worship culminates in the supreme labour, and even sorrow, of real prayer. This is man at his utmost; and it has for it near neighbours all the great things that men or nations do. But when a nation must go to righteous war it embarks on one of the very greatest acts of its life, especially if its very existence as a servant of God's kingdom hang on it. A state of war is really the vast and prolonged act of a corporate soul, with a number of minor acts organized into it. It is capable of being offered to a God whose kingdom is a public campaign moving through history, and coming by the faith, toil, peril, sacrifice, grief, and glory of nations, as well as the hearts and souls. It is not possible to separate moral acts so great and solemn as the act of prayer (especially common and corporate prayer) and the act of war; nor to think them severed in the movement, judgment, and purpose of the Eternal. And we are forced into paradox again. The deeper we go down into the valley of decision the higher we must rise (if we are to possess and command our souls) into the mount of prayer, and we must hold up the hands of those whose chief concern is to prevail with God. If we win we shall have a new sense of power amid all our loss and weakness; but what we shall need most of all if the power to use that power, and to protest us from our victory and its perilous sequels, whether of pride or poverty. And if we do not win we shall need it more. There will be much to sober us either way, more perhaps than ever before in our history.

But that is not all, and it is not enough. As Christian people we need something to sanctify that very sobering and to do for the new moral thoughtfulness itself what that does for the peace-bred levity of the natural man. For such a purpose there is no agent like prayer--serious, thinking, private prayer, or prayer in groups, in small, grave, congenial, understanding groups--prayer with the historic sense, church-nurtured and Bible-fed. Public prayer by all means, but, apart from liturgical form, the more open the occasions and the larger the company the more hard it may be to secure for such prayer the right circumstances or the right lead. Public facility is apt to outstrip the real intimacy and depth with God. While on the other hand, the prayer that freely rises and aptly flows in our audience of God may be paralyzed in an audience of men. So that public prayer does not always reflect the practice of private petition as the powerful factor it is in

Christian life and history. It does not always suggest a door opened in heaven, the insight or fellowship of eternal yet historic powers in awful orbits. It does not always do justice to our best private prayer, to private prayer made a business and suffused with as much sacred mind as goes to the more secular side even of the Christian life. Should ministers enlist? it is asked. But to live in true and concrete prayer is to be a combatant in the War, as well as a statesman after it, if statesmen ought to see the whole range of forces at work. The saintly soldier still needs the soldier saint. Yet so much prayer has ceased to be a matter of thought, will, or conflict, and religion therefore has become so otiose, that it is not easy even for the Christian public to take such a saying as more than a phrase. This is but one expression of a general scepticism, both in the Church and out, about prayer, corporate or private, as power with God, and therefore as momentous in the affairs of life and history. But momentous and effectual it must be. Other things being equal, a voluntary and convinced army is worth more than a conscript one. So to know that we are morally right means worlds for our shaping of the things that face us and must be met; and we are never so morally right as in proficient prayer with the Holy One and the Just. It has, therefore, a vast effect on the course of things if we believe at all in their moral destiny. More it wrought by it than the too wise world wots; and all the more as it is the prayer of a great soul or a great Church. It is a power behind thrones, and it neutralizes, at the far end, the visible might of armies and their victories. It settles at last whether morality or machinery is to rule the world. If it lose battles, it wins in the long historic campaign. Whereas, if we have no such action with God, we lose delicacy of perception in the finer forces of affairs; we are out of touch and understanding with the final control in things, the power that is working to the top always; we become dense in regard to the subtle but supreme influences that take the generals and chancellors by surprise; and we are at the mercy of the sleepless action of the kingdom of evil on the world. It is a fatal thing to under estimate the enemy; and it is in Christian prayer, seriously and amply pursued, that the soul really learns to gauge evil's awful and superhuman power in affairs. I am speaking not only of the single soul, perhaps at the moment not chiefly, but of the soul and prayer of a society like the true Church or a sobered people. The real power of prayer in history is not a fusillade of praying units of whom Christ is the chief, but it is the corporate action of a Saviour-Intercessor and His community, a volume and energy of prayer organized in a Holy Spirit and in the Church the Spirit creates. The saints shall thus judge the world and control life. Neither for the individual nor for the Church is true prayer an enclave in life's larger and more actual course. It is not a sacred enclosure, a lodge in some vast wilderness. That is the weak side of pietism. But, however intimate, it is in the most organic and vital context of affairs, private and public, if all things work together, deeply and afar, for the deep and final kingdom of God. Its constant defeat of our egoism means the victory of our social unity and its weal. For the egoist neither prays nor loves. On the other hand, such prayer recalls us from a distraught altruism, teeming with oddities, and frayed down to atomism by the variety of calls upon it; because the prayer is the supreme energy of a loving will and believing soul engaged with the Love that binds the earth, the sun, and all the stars. So far it is from being the case that love to God has no sphere outside love to man that our love to man perishes unless it is fed by the love that spends itself on God in prayer, and is lifted thereby to a place and a sway not historic only, but cosmic.

Our communion with God in Christ rose, and it abides, in a crisis which shook not the earth only, but also heaven, in a tragedy and victory more vast, awful, and pregnant than the greatest war in history could be. Therefore the prayer which gives us an ever-deeper interest and surer insight into that eternal moral crisis of the Cross gives us also (though it might take generations) a footing that commands all the losses or victories of earth, and a power that rules both spirit and conscience in the clash and crash of worlds. As there is devoted thought which ploughs its way into the command of Nature, there is thought, still more devoted, that prays itself into that moral interior of the Cross, where the kingdom of God is founded once for all on the last principle and power of the universe, and set up, not indeed amid the wreck of civilization, but by its new birth and a baptism so as by fire. Prayer of the right kind, with heart and soul and strength and mind, unites any society in which it prevails with those last powers of moral and social regeneration that settle history and that reside in the creative grace of the Cross, which is God's true omnipotence in the world. "O God, who showest Thine almighty power most chiefly in having mercy and forgiving." Such speech as this may to some appear tall and rhetorical; but it would have so seemed to no father of the church, ancient or modern, taking apostolic measure of the place and moment of Christ in society, history, or the universe.

If war is in any sense God's judgment on sin, and if sin was destroyed by the judgment in Christ and on Him, let us pray with a new depth and significance to-day, "O Lamb of God, that takest away the sin of the world, grant us Thy peace. Send us the peace that honours in act and deed that righteous and final judgment in Thy Cross of all historic things, and that makes therein for Thy Kingdom on earth as in heaven. Give peace in our time, O Lord, but, peace or war, Take the crown of this poor world."

CHAPTER V

The Ceaselessness of Prayer

Prayer as Christian freedom, and prayer as Christian life--these are two points I would now expand.

I. First, as to the moral freedom involved and achieved in prayer.

Prayer has been described as religion in action. But that as it stands is not a sufficient definition of the prayer which lives on the Cross. The same thing might be said about the choicest forms of Christian service to humanity. It is true enough, and it may carry us far; but only if we become somewhat clear about the nature of the religion at work. Prayer is certainly not the action of a religion mainly subjective. It is the effective work of a religion which hangs upon the living God, of a soul surer of God than of itself, and living not its own life, but the life of the Son of God. To say prayer is faith in action would be better; for the word "faith" carries a more objective reference than the word "religion." Faith is faith in another. In prayer we do not so much work as interwork. We are fellow workers with God in a reciprocity. And as God is the freest Being in existence, such co-operant prayer is the freest things that man can do. It we were free in sinning, how much more free in the praying which undoes sin! If we were free to break God's will, how much more free to turn it or to accept it! Petitionary prayer is man's cooperation in kind with God amidst a world He freely made for freedom. The world was made by a freedom which not only left room for the kindred freedom of prayer, but which so ordered all things in its own interest that in their deepest depths they conspire to produce prayer. To pray in faith is to answer God's freedom in its own great note. It means we are taken up into the fundamental movement of the world. It is to realize that for which the whole world, the world as a whole, was made. It is an earnest of the world's consummation. We are doing what the whole world was created to do. We overleap in the spirit all between now and then, as in the return to Jesus we overleap the two thousand years that intervene. The object the Father's loving purpose had in appointing the whole providential order was intercourse with man's soul. That order of the world is, therefore, no rigid fixture, nor is it even a fated evolution. It is elastic, adjustable, flexible, with margins for freedom, for free modification in God and man; always keeping in view that final goal of communion, and growing into it be a spiritual interplay in which the whole of Nature is involved. The goal of the whole cosmic order is the "manifestation of the sons of God," the realization of complete sonship, its powers and its confidences.

Thus we rise to say that our prayer is the momentary function of the Eternal Son's communion and intercession with the Eternal Father. We are integrated in advance into the final Christ, for whom, and to whom, all creation moves. Our prayer is more than the acceptance by us of God's will; it is its assertion in us. The will of God is that men should pray everywhere. He wills to be entreated. Prayer is that will of God's making itself good. When we entreat we give effect to His dearest will. And in His will is our eternal liberty. In this will of His our finds itself, and is at home. It ranges the liberties of the Father's house. But here prayer must draw from the Cross, which is the frontal act of our emancipation as well as the central revelation of God's own freedom in grace. The action of the Atonement and of its release of us is in the nature of prayer. It is the free return of the Holy upon the Holy in the Great Reconciliation.

II. Then, secondly, as to prayer being the expression of the perennial new life of faith in the Cross. The Christian life is prayer without ceasing.

When we are told to pray without ceasing, it seems to many tastes to-day to be somewhat extravagant language. And no doubt that is true. Why should we be concerned to deny it? Measured language and the elegant mean is not the note of the New Testament at least. Mhoen zyan, said the Greek--too much of nothing. But can we love or trust God too much? Christian faith is one that overcomes and commands the world in a passion rather than balances it. It triumphs in a conclusive bliss, it does not play off one part against another. The grace of Christ is not but graciousness of nature, and He does not rule His Church by social act. The peace of God is not the calm of culture, it is not the charm of breeding. Every great forward movement in Christianity is associated with much that seems academically extravagant. Erasmus is always shocked with Luther. It is only an outlet of that essential extravagance which makes the paradox of the Cross, and keeps it as the irritant, no less than the life of the world--perhaps because it is the life of the world. There is nothing so abnormal, so unworldly, so supernatural, in human life as prayer, nothing that is more of an instinct, it is true, but also nothing that is less rational among all the things that keep above the level of the silly. The whole Christian life in so far as it is lived from the Cross and by the Cross is rationally an extravagance. For the Cross is the paradox of all things; and the action of the Spirit is the greatest miracle in the world; and yet it is the principle of the world. Paradox is but the expression of that dualism which is the moral foundation of a Christian world. I live who die daily. I live another's life.

To pray without ceasing is not, of course, to engage in prayer without break. That is an impossible literalism. True, "They rest not day and night, saying, Holy, holy, holy, Lord God Almighty, who wert, and art, and art to come." But it is mere poverty of soul to think of this as the iteration of a doxology. It is deep calling unto deep, eternity greeting eternity. The only answer to God's eternity is an eternal attitude of prayer.

Nor does the phrase mean that the Church shall use careful means that the stream and sound of prayer shall never cease to flow at some spots of the earth, as the altar lamp goes not out. It does not mean the continuous murmur of the mass following the sun round the world, incessant relays of adoring priests, and functions going on day and night.

But it means the constant bent and drift of the soul--as the Word which was from the beginning (John i. 1) was hroe ton Qesn. All the current of its being set towards Him. It means being "in Christ," being in such a moving, returning Christ--reposing in this godward, and not merely godlike life. The note of prayer becomes the habit of the heart, the tone and tension of its new nature; in such a way that when we are released from the grasp of our occupations the soul rebounds to its true bent, quest, and even pressure upon God. It is the soul's habitual appetite and habitual food. A growing child of God is always hungry. Prayer is not identical with the occasional act of praying. Like the act of faith, it is a whole life thought of as action. It is the life of faith in its purity, in its vital action. Eating and speaking are necessary to life, but they are not living. And how hidden prayer may be--beneath even gaiety! If you look down on Portland Race you see but a shining sea; only the pilot knows the tremendous current that pervades the smiling calm.

So far this "pray without ceasing" from being absurd because extravagant that every man's life is in some sense a continual state of prayer. For what is his life's prayer but its ruling passion? All energies, ambitions and passions are but expressions of a standing nisus in life, of a hunger, a draft, a practical demand upon the future, upon the unattained and the unseen. Every life is a draft upon the unseen. If you are not praying towards God you are towards something else. You pray as your face is set--towards Jerusalem or Babylon. The very egotism of craving life is prayer. The great difference is the object of it. To whom, for what, do we pray? The man whose passion is habitualy set upon pleasure, knowledge, wealth, honour, or power is in a state of prayer to these things or for them. He prays without ceasing. These are his real gods, on whom he waits day and night. He may from time to time go on his knees in church, and use words of Christian address and petition. He may even feel a momentary unction in so doing. But it is a flicker; the other devotion is his steady flame. His real God is the ruling passion and steady pursuit of his life taken as a whole. He certainly does not pray in the name of Christ. And what he worships in spirit and in truth is another God than he addresses at religious times. He prays to an unknown God for a selfish boon. Still, in a sense, he prays. The set and drift of his nature prays. It is the prayer of instinct, not of faith. It is prayer that needs total conversion. But he cannot stop praying either to God or to

God's rival--to self, society, world, flesh, or even devil. Every life that is not totally inert in praying either to God or God's adversary.

What do we really mean, whom do we mean, when we say, "My God"? In what sense mine? May our God not be but an idol we exploit, and in due course our doom?

There is a fearful and wonderful passage in Kierkegaard's *Entweder-Oder* which, if we transfer it to this connection, stirs thoughts deeper than its own tragedy. The seduced, heart-broken, writes to the seducer.

"John! I do not say my John. That I now see you never were. I am heavily punished for ever letting such an idea be my joy. Yet--yet, mine you are--my seducer, my deceiver, my enemy, my murderer, the spring of my calamity, the grave of my joy, the abyss of my misery. I call you mine, and I am yours--your curse for ever. Oh, do not think I will slay you and put a dagger into you. But flee where you will, I am yours, to the earth's end yours. Love a hundred others but I am yours. I am yours in your last hour, I am yours, yours, yours--your curse."

Beware lest the whole trend of the soul fix on a diety that turns a doom. There is the prayer which makes God our judgment as well as one which makes Him our joy.

Prayer is the nature of our hell as well as our heaven.

Our hell is ceaseless, passionate, fruitless, hopeless, gnawing prayer. It is the heart churning, churning grinding itself out in misery. It is life's passion and struggle surging back on itself like a barren, salt, corroding sea. It is the heart's blood rising like a fountain only to fall back on us in red rain. It is prayer which we cannot stop, addressed to nothing, and obtaining nothing. It calls into space and night. Or it is addressed to self, and it aggravates the wearing action of self on self. Our double being revolves on itself, like two millstones with nothing to grind.

And prayer is our heaven. It goes home to God, and attains there, and rests there. We are "in Christ," whose whole existence is prayer, who is wholly prsz tsn Qesn for us. He is there to extinguish our hell and make our heaven--far more to quench our wrath and our seething than God's.

To cultivate the ceaseless spirit of prayer, use more frequent acts of prayer. To learn to pray with freedom, force yourself to pray. The great liberty begins in necessity.

Do not say, "I cannot pray, I am not in the spirit." Pray till you are in the spirit. Think of analogies from lower levels. Sometimes when you need rest most you are too restless to lie down and take it. Then compel yourself to lie down, and to lie still. Often in ten minutes the compulsion fades into consent, and you sleep, and rise a new man.

Again, it is often hard enough to take up the task which in half an hour you enjoy. It is often against the grain to turn out of an evening to meet the friends you promised. But once you are in their midst you are in your element.

Sometimes, again, you say, "I will not go to church. I do not feel that way." That is where the habit of an ordered religious life comes in aid. Religion is the last region for chance desires. Do it as a duty, and it may open out as a blessing. Omit it, and you may miss the one thing that would have made an eternal difference. You stroll instead, and return with nothing but appetite--when you might have come back with an inspiration. Compel yourself to meet your God as you would meet your promises, your obligations, your fellow men.

So if you are averse to pray, pray the more. Do not call it lip-service. That is not the lip-service God disowns. It is His Spirit acting in your self-coercive will, only not yet in your heart. What is unwelcome to God is lip-service which is untroubled at not being more. As appetite comes with eating, so prayer with praying. Our hearts learn the language of the lips.

Compel yourself often to shape on your lips the detailed needs of your soul. It is not needful to inform God, but to deepen you, to inform yourself before God, to enrich that intimacy with ourself which is so necessary to answer the intimacy of God. To common sense the fact that God knows all we need, and wills us all good, the fact of His infinite Fatherhood, is a reason for not praying. Why tell Him what He knows? Why ask what He is more than willing to give? But to Christian faith and to spiritual reason it is just the other way. Asking is polar cooperation. Jesus turned the fact to a use exactly the contrary of its deistic sense. He made the all-knowing Fatherhood the ground of true prayer. We do not ask as beggars but as children. Petition is not mere receptivity, nor is it mere pressure; it is filial reciprocity. Love loves to be told what it knows already. Every lover knows that. It wants to be asked for what it longs to give. And that is the principle of prayer to the all-knowing Love. As God knows all, you may reckon that your brief and humble prayer will be understood (Matt. vi. 8). It will be taken up into the intercession of the Spirit stripped of its dross, its inadequacy made good, and presented as prayer should be. That is praying in the Holy Ghost. Where should you carry your burden but to the Father, where Christ took the burden of all the world? We tell God, the heart searcher, our heavy thoughts to escape from brooding over them. "When my spirit was overwhelmed within me, Thou knewest my path." (Ps. cxlii. 3). So Paul says the Spirit intercedes for us and gives our broken prayer divine effect (Rom. viii. 26). To be sure of God's sympathy is to be inspired to prayer, where His mere knowledge would crush it. There is no father who would be satisfied that his son should take everything and ask for nothing. It would be thankless. To cease asking is to cease to be grateful. And what kills petition kills praise.

Go into your chamber, shut the door, and cultivate the habit of praying audibly. Write prayers and burn them. Formulate your soul. Pay no attention to literary form, only to spiritual reality. Read a passage of Scripture and then sit down and turn it into prayer, written or spoken. Learn to be particular, specific, and detailed in your prayer so long as you are not trivial. General prayers, literary prayers, and stately phrases are, for private prayer, traps and sops to the soul. To formulate your soul is one valuable means to escape formalizing it. This is the best, the wholesome, kind of self-examination. Speaking with God discovers us safely to ourselves We "find" ourselves, come to ourselves, in the Spirit. Face your special weaknesses and sins before God. Force yourself to say to God exactly where you are wrong. When anything goes wrong, do not ask to have it set right, without asking in prayer what is was in you that made it go wrong. It is somewhat fruitless to ask for a general grace to help specific flaws, sins, trials, and griefs. Let prayer be concrete, actual, a direct product of life's real experiences. Pray as your actual self, not as some fancied saint. Let it be closely relevant to your real situation. Pray without ceasing in this sense. Pray without a break between your prayer and your life. Pray so that there is a real continuity between your prayer and your whole actual life. But I will bear round upon this point again immediately.

Meantime, let me say this. Do not allow your practice in prayer to be arrested by scientific or philosophic considerations as to how answer is possible. That is a valuable subject for discussion, but it is not entitled to control our practice. Faith is at least as essential to the soul as science, and it has a foundation more independent. And prayer is not only a necessity of faith, it is faith itself in action.

Criticism of prayer dissolves in the experience of it. When the soul is at close quarters with God it becomes enlarged enough to hold together in harmony things that oppose, and to have room for harmonious contraries. For instance: God, of course, is always working for His Will and Kingdom. But man is bound to pray for its coming, while it is coming all the time. Christ laid stress on prayer as a necessary means of bringing the Kingdom to pass. And it cannot come without our praying. Why? Because its coming is the prayerful frame of soul. So again with God's freedom. It is absolute. But it reckons on ours. Our prayer does not force His hand; it answers His freedom in kind. We are never so active and free as in prayer to an absolutely free God. We share His freedom when we are "in Christ."

If I must choose between Christ, who bids me pray for everything, and the servant, who tells me certain answers are physically and rationally impossible, must I not choose Christ? Because, while the savant knows much about nature and its action (and much more than Christ did), Christ knew everything about the God of nature and His reality. He knew more of what is possible to God than anybody has ever known about what is possible in nature. On such a subject as prayer, anyone is a greater authority who wholly knows the will of God than he who only knows

God's methods, and knows them but in part. Prayer is not an act of knowledge but of faith. It is not a matter of calculation but of confidence--"that our faith should not stand in the wisdom of men, but in the power of God." Which means that in this region we are not to be regulated by science, but by God's self-revelation. Do not be so timid about praying wrongly if you pray humbly. If God is really the Father that Christ revealed, then the principle is--take everything to Him that exercises you. Apart from frivolity, such as praying to find the stud you lost, or the knife, or the umbrella, there is really no limitation in the New Testament on the contents of petition. Any regulation is as to the spirit of the prayer, the faith it springs from. In all distress which mars your peace, petition must be the form your faith takes--petition for rescue. Keep close to the New Testament Christ, and then ask for anything you desire in that contact. Ask for everything you can ask in Christ's name, i.e. everything desirable by a man who is in Christ's kingdom of God, by a man who lives for it at heart, everything in tune with the purpose and work of the kingdom in Christ. If you are in that kingdom, then pray freely for whatever you need or wish to keep you active and effective for it, from daily bread upwards and outwards. In all things make your requests known. At least you have laid them on God's heart; and faith means confidences between you and not only favours. And there is not confidence if you keep back what is hot or heavy on your heart. If prayer is not a play of the religious fantasy, or a routine task, it must be the application of faith to a concrete actual and urgent situation. Only remember that prayer does not work by magic, and that stormy desire is not fervent, effectual prayer. You may be but exploiting a mighty power; whereas you must be in real contact with the real God. It is the man that most really has God that most really seeks God.

I said a little while ago that to pray without ceasing also meant to pray without a breach with your actual life and the whole situation in which you are. This is the point at which to dwell on that. If you may not come to God with the occasions of your private life and affairs, then there is some unreality in the relation between you and Him. If some private crisis absorbs you, some business or family anxiety of little moment to others but of much to you, and if you may not bring that to God in prayer, then one of two things. Either it is not you, in your actual reality, that came to God, but it is you in a pose--you in some role which you are trying with poor success to play before Him. You are trying to pray as another person than you are,--a better person, perhaps, as some great apostle, who should have on his worshipping mind nothing but the grand affairs of the Church and Kingdom, and not be worried by common cares. You are praying in court-dress. You are trying to pray as you imagine one should pray to God, i.e. as another person than you are, and in other circumstances. You are creating a self and a situation to place before

God. Either that or you are not praying to a God who loves, helps, and delivers you in every pinch of life, but only to one who uses you as a pawn for the victory of His great kingdom. You are not praying to Christ's God. You are praying to a God who cares only for the great actions in His kingdom, for the heroic people who cherish nothing but the grand style, or for the calm people who do not deeply feel life's trials. The reality of prayer is bound up with the reality and intimacy of life.

And its great object is to get home as we are to God as He is, and to win response even when we get no compliance. The prayer of faith does not mean a prayer absolutely sure that it will receive what it asks. That is not faith. Faith is that attitude of soul and self to God which is the root and reservoir of prayer apart from all answer. It is what turns need into request. It is what moves your need to need God. It is what makes you sure your prayer is heard and stored, whether granted or not. "He putteth all my tears in His bottle." God has old prayers of yours long maturing by Him. What wine you will drink with Him in His kingdom! Faith is sure that God refuses with a smile; that He says No in the spirit of Yes, and He gives or refuses always in Christ, our Great Amen. And better prayers are stirred by the presence of the Deliverer than even by the need of deliverance.

It is not sufficiently remembered that before prayer can expect an answer it must be itself an answer. That is what is meant by prayer in the name of Christ. It is prayer which answers God's gift in Christ, with Whom are already given us all things. And that is why we must pray without ceasing, because in Christ God speaks without ceasing. Natural or instinctive prayer is one thing; supernatural prayer is another; it is the prayer not of instinct but of faith. It is our word answering God's. It is more the prayer of fullness even than of need, of strength than of weakness--though it be "a strength girt round with weakness." Prayer which arises from mere need is flung out to a power which is only remembered, or surmised, or unknown. It is flung into darkness and uncertainty. But in Christian prayer we ask for what we need because we are full of faith in God's power and word, because need becomes petition at the touch of His word. (I always feel that in the order of our public worship prayer should immediately follow the lesson, without the intrusion on an anthem. And for the reason I name--that Christian prayer is our word answering God's). We pray, therefore, in Christ's name, or for His sake, because we pray as answering the gift in Christ. Our prayer is the note the tremulous soul utters when its chords are smitten by Him. We then answer above all things God's prayer to us in His cross that we would be reconciled. God so beseeches us in Christ. So that, if we put it strongly, we may say that our prayer to God in Christ is our answer to God's prayer to us there. "The best thing in prayer is faith," says Luther.

And the spirit of prayer in Christ's name is the true child-spirit. A certain type of religion is fond of dwelling on faith as the spirit of divine childhood; and its affinities are all with the tender and touching element in childhood. But one does not always get from the prophets of such piety the impression of a life breathed in prayer. And the notion is not the New Testament sense of being children of God. That is a manlier, a maturer thing. It is being sons of God by faith, and by faith's energy of prayer. It is not the sense of being as helpless as a child that clings, not the sense of weakness, ignorance, gentleness, and all that side of things. But it is the spirit of a prayer which is a great act of faith, and therefore a power. Faith is not simply surrender, but adoring surrender, not a mere sense of dependence, but an act of intelligent committal, and the confession of a holiness which is able to save, keep, and bless for ever.

How is it that the experience of life is so often barren of spiritual culture for religious people? They become stoic and stalwart, but not humble; they have been sight, but no insight. Yet it is not the stalwarts but the saints that judge the world, i.e. that ake the true divine measure of the world and get to its subtle, silent, and final powers. Whole sections of our Protestantism have lost the virtue of humility or the understanding of it. It means for them no more than modesty or diffidence. It is the humility of weakness, not of power. To many useful, and even strong, people no experience seems to bring this subtle, spiritual intelligence, this finer discipline of the moral man. No rebukes, no rebuffs, no humiliations, no sorrows, seem to bring it to them. They have no spiritual history.

Their spiritual biography not even an angel could write. There is no romance in their soul's story. At sixty they are, spiritually, much where they were at twenty-six. To calamity, to discipline of any kind, they are simply resilient. Their religion is simply elasticity. It is but lusty life. They rise up after the smart is over, or the darkness fades away, as self-confident as if they were but seasoned politicians beaten at one election, but sure of doing better at the next. They are to the end just irrepressible, or persevering, or dogged. And they are as juvenile in moral insight, as boyish in spiritual perception, as ever.

Is it not because they have never really had personal religion? That is, they have never really prayed with all their heart; only, at most, with all their fervour, certainly not with strength and mind. They have neer "spread out" their whole soul and situation to a god who knows. They have never opened the petals of their soul in the warm sympathy of His knowledge. They have not become particular enough in their prayer, faithful with themselves, or relevant to their complete situation. They do not face themselves, only what happens to them. They pray with their heart and not with their conscience. They pity themselves, perhaps they spare themselves, they shrink from hurting themselves more than misfortune hurts them. They say, "If you knew all you could not help pitying me." They do not say, "God knows all, and how can He spare me?" For themselves, or for their fellows, it is the prayer of pity, not of repentance. We need the prayer of self-judgment more than the prayer of fine insight.

We are not humble in God's sight, partly because in our prayer there is a point at which we cease to pray, where we do not turn everything out into God's light. It is because there is a chamber or two in our souls where we do not enter in and take God with us. We hurry Him by the door as we take Him along the corridors of our life to see our tidy places or our public rooms. We ask from our prayers too exclusively comfort, strength, enjoyment, or tenderness and graciousness, and not often enough humiliation and its fine strength. We want beautiful prayers, touching prayers, simple prayers, thoughtful prayers; prayers with a quaver or a tear in them, or prayers with delicacy and dignity in them. But searching prayer, humbling prayer, which is the prayer of the conscience, and not merely of the heart or taste; prayer which is bent on reality, and to win the new joy goes through new misery if need by--are such prayers as welcome and common as they should be? Too much of our prayer is apt to leave us with the self-complacency of the sympathetically incorrigible, of the benevolent and irremediable, of the breezy octogenarian, all of whose yesterdays look backward with a cheery and exasperating smile.

It is an art--this great and creative prayer--this intimate conversation with God. *"Magna ars est conversari cum Deo,"* says Thomas a Kempis. It has to be learned. In social life we learn that conversation is not mere talk. There is an art in it, if we are not to have a table of gabblers. How much more is it so in the conversation of heaven! We must learn that art by practice, and by keeping the best society in that kind. Associate much with the great masters in this kind; especially with the Bible; and chiefly with Christ. Cultivate His Holy Spirit. He is the grand master of God's art and mystery in communing with man. And there is no other teacher, at least, of man's art of communion with God.

CHAPTER VI

The Vicariousness of Prayer

I

The work of the ministry labours under one heavy disadvantage when we regard it as a profession and compare it with other professions. In these, experience brings facility, a sense of mastery in the subject, self-satisfaction, self-confidence; but in our subject the more we pursue it, the more we enter into it, so much the more are we cast down with the overwhelming sense, not only of our insufficiency, but of our unworthiness. Of course, in the technique of our work we acquire a certain ease. We learn to speak more or less freely and aptly. We learn the knack of handling a text, of conducting church work, or dealing with men, and the life. If it were only texts or men we had to handle! But we have to handle the gospel. We have to lift up Christ--a Christ who is the death of natural self-confidence--a humiliating, even a crushing Christ; and we are not always alive to our uplifting and resurrection in Him. We have to handle a gospel that is a new rebuke to us every step we gain in intimacy with it. There is no real intimacy with the gospel which does not mean a new sense of God's holiness, and it may be long before we realize that the same holiness that condemns is that which saves. There is no new insight into the Cross which does not bring, whatever else come with it, a deeper sense of the solemn holiness of the love that meets us there. And there is no new sense of the holy God that does not arrest His name upon our unclean lips. If our very repentance is to be repented of, and we should be forgiven much in our very prayers, how shall we be proud, or even pleased, with what we may think a success in our preaching? So that we are not surprised that some preachers, after what the public calls a most brilliant and impressive discourse, retire (as the emperor retired to close his life in the cloister) to humble themselves before God, to ask forgiveness for the poor message, and to call themselves most unprofitable servants--yea, even when they knew themselves that they had "done well." The more we grasp our gospel the more it abashes us.

Moreover, as we learn more of the seriousness of the gospel for the human soul, we feel the more that every time we present it we are adding to the judgment of some as well as to the salvation of others. We are not like speakers who present a matter that men can freely take or leave, where they can agree or differ with us without moral result. No true preacher can be content that his flock should believe in him. That were egoism. They must believe with him. The deeper and surer our gospel is the more is our work a judgment on those to whom it is not a grace. This was what bore upon the Saviour's own soul, and darkened His very agony into eclipse. That He, who knew Himself to be the salvation of His own beloved people, should, by His very love, become their doom! And here we watch and suffer with Him, however sleepily. There is put into our charge our dear people's life or death. For to those to whom we are not life we are death, in proportion as we truly preach, not ourselves, but the real salvation of Christ.

How solemn our place is! It is a sacramental place. We have not simply to state our case, we have to convey our Christ, and to convey Him effectually as the soul's final fate. We are sacramental elements, broken often, in the Lord's hands, as He dispenses His grace through us. We do not, of course, believe that orders are an ecclesiastical sacrament, as Rome does. But we are forced to realize the idea underlying that dogma--the sacramental nature of our person, work, and vocation for the gospel. We are not saviours. There is only one Saviour. But we are His sacraments. We do not believe in an ecclesiastical priesthood; but we are made to feel how we stand between God and the people as none of our flock do. We bring Christ to them, and them to Christ, in sacrificial action in a way far more moral, inward, and taxing than official preisthood can be. As ministers we lead the sacerdotal function of the whole Church in the world--its holy confession and sacrifice for the world in Christ.

We ought, indeed, to feel the dignity of the ministry; we must present some protest against the mere fraternal conception which so easily sinks into an unspiritual familiarity. But still more than the dignity of the ministry do its elect feel its solemnity. How can it be otherwise? We have to dwell much with the everlasting burnings of God's love. We have to tend that consuming fire. We have to feed our life where all the tragedy of life is gathered to an infinite and victorious crisis in Christ. We are not the fire, but we live where it burns. The matter we handle in our theological thought we can only handle with some due protection for our face. It is one of the dangerous industries. It is continually acting on us, continually searching our inner selves that no part of us may be unforgiven, unfed, or unsanctified. We cannot hold it and examine it at arm's length. It enters into us. It evokes the perpetual comment of our souls, and puts us continually on self-judgment. Our critic, our judge, is at the door. Self-condemnation arrests denunciation. And the true apostle can never condemn but in the spirit of self-condemnation.

But, after all, our doom is our blessing. Our Judge is on our side. For if humiliation be wrung from us, still more is faith, hope, and prayer. Everything that rebukes our self-satisfaction does still more to draw out our faith. When we are too tired or doubtful to ask we can praise and adore. When we are weary of confessing our sin we can forget ourselves in a godly sort and confess our Saviour. We can say the creed when we cannot raise the song. He also hath given us the reconciliation. The more judgment we see in the holy cross the more we see it is judgment unto salvation. The more we are humbled the more we "roll our souls upon Christ." And we recover our self-possession only by giving our soul again and again to Christ to keep. We win a confidence in self-despair. Prayer is given us as wings wherewith to mount, but also to shield our face when they have carried us before the great white throne. It is in prayer that the holiness comes home as love, and the love is established as holiness. At every step our thought is transformed to prayer, and our prayer opens new ranges of thought. His great revelation is His holiness, always outgoing in atoning love. The Christian revelation is not "God is love" so much as "love is God." That is, it is not God's love, but the infinite power of God's love, its finality, omnipotence, and absoluteness. It is not passionate and helpless love, but it has power to subdue everything that rises against it. And that is the holiness of love--the eternal thing in it. We receive the last reconciliation. Then the very wrath of God becomes a glory. The red in the sky is the new dawn. Our self-accusation becomes a new mode of praise. Our loaded hearts spring light again. Our heavy conscience turns to grave moral power. A new love is born for our kind. A new and tender patience steals upon us. We see new ways of helping, serving, and saving. We issue into a new world. We are one with the Christ not only on His cross, but in His resurrection. Think of the resurrection power and calm, of that solemn final peace, that infinite satisfaction in the eternal thing eternally achieved, which filled His soul when He had emerged from death, when man's worst had been done, and God's best had been won, for ever and for all. We have our times of entrance into that Christ. As we were one with Him in the likeness of His death, so we are in the likeness of His resurrection. And the same Eternal Spirit which puts the preacher's soul much upon the cross also raises it continually from the dead. We overcome our mistakes, negligences, sins; nay, we rise above the sin of the whole world, which will not let our souls be as good as they are. We overcome the world, and take courage, and are of new cheer. We are in the Spirit. And then we can preach, pray, teach, heal. And even the unclean lips then put a new thrill into our sympathy and a new tremor into our praise.

If it be not so, how shall our dangerous work not demoralize us, and we perish from our too much contact with holy things.

The minister's holiest prayer is hardly lawful to utter. Few of his public would comprehend it. Some would dismiss it with their most opprobrious word. They would call it theological. When he calls to God in his incomprehensible extremity they would translate it into an appeal to Elijah (Matt. xxvii. 47). For to them theology is largely mythology.

We are called at the present day to a reconstruction of the old theology, a restatement of the old gospel. We have to reappropriate and remint the truth of our experienced Christianity. But what a hardship it is that this call should search us at a time when the experimental power of our Christianity has abated, and the evangelical experience is so low and so confused as it often is! It must be the minister's work to recover and deepen this experience for the churches, in the interest of faith, and of the truth in which faith renders account of itself. Theological inadequacy, and especially antagonism to theology, means at root religious defect. For the reformation of belief we must have a restoration of faith. And a chief engine for such recovery of faith is for us what it was for Luther and his like--prayer. And it is not mindless prayer, but that prayer which is the wrestling of the conscience and not merely the cry of the heart, the prayer for reconciliation and redemption and not merely for guidance and comfort, the prayer of faith and not merely of love.

I saw in a friend's house a photograph from (I think) Durer--just two tense hands, palms together, and lifted in prayer. It was most eloquent, most subduing. I wish I could stamp the picture on the page here and fit it to Milton's line:

> The great two-handed engine at our door.[5]

II

Public prayer is, on the whole, the most difficult part of the work of the minister. To help the difficulty I have always claimed that pulpit notes of prayer may be used. "The Lord's Prayer" itself is of this nature. It is not a prayer, but a scheme of prayer, heads of prayer, or buoys in the channel. But even with the use of all helps there are perils enough. There are prayers that, in the effort to become real, are much too familiar in their fashion of speech. A young man began his prayer, in my own hearing, with the words, "O God, we have come to have a chat with Thee." It was gruesome. Think of it as a sample of modern piety for the young! No prayers, certainly no public prayers, should be "chats with God." Again, other prayers are sentimental prayers. George Dawson's volume has this fault. The prayers of the Church should not be exposures of the affectional man. The public prayer of the Church, as the company of grace, is the saved soul returning to God that gave it; it is the sinner coming to the Saviour, or the ransomed of the Lord returning to Zion; it is the sanctified with the sanctifier; it is not primarily the child talking to the Father--though that note may prevail in more private prayers. We are more than stray sheep reclaimed. We are those whose defiant iniquity has lain upon Christ for us all.

But the root of the difficulty of public prayer lies further back than in the matter of style. It lies in the difficulty of private prayer, in its spiritual poverty, its inertia, its anemia. What culture can deal with the rooted difficulty that resides there, out of sight, in the inner man of the heart, for lack of the courage of faith, for sheer spiritual fecklessness? Yet the preparation for prayer is to pray. The prayer is the practice of prayer. It is only prayer that teaches to pray. The minister ought never to speak before men in God's name without himself first speaking to God in man's name, and making intercession as for himself so for his people.

Intercession! We are properly vigilant that the minister do not sever himself from his people in any sacredotal way. But for all that, is the minister's personal and private prayer on exactly the same footing as a layman's? It is a question that leads to the distinction between intercessory and vicarious prayer. The personal religion of the minister is vicarious even when it is not intercessory. Great indeed is the spiritual value of private intercession. The intercessory private prayer of the minister is the best corrective of the critical spirit or the grumbling spirit which so easily besets and withers us to-day. That reconciliation, that pacification of heart, which comes by prayer opens in us a fountain of private intercession, especially for our antagonists. Only, of course, it must be private. But the minister is also praying to his people's good even when he is not interceeding on their behalf, or leading them in prayer. What he is for his Church he is with his whole personality. And so his private and personal prayers are vicarious for his people even when he does not know it. No Christian man lives for himself, nor believes for himself. And if the private Christian in his private prayers does not pray, any more than he lives, unto himself alone, much more is this true for the minister. His private prayers make a great difference to his people. They may not know what makes his spell and blessing; even he may not. But it is his most private prayers; which, thus, are vicarious even where not intercessory.

What he is for his Church, I have said, he is with his whole personality. And nothing gives us personality like true prayer. Nothing makes a man so original. We cannot be true Christians without being original. Living faith destroys the commonplaceness, the monotony of life. Are not all men original in death? *"Je mourrai seul."* Much more are they original and their true selves in Christ's death, and in their part and lot in that. For true originality we must be one, and closely one, with God. To be creative we must learn with the Creator. The most effectual man in history was he who said, "I live; yet not I, but Christ liveth in me." What a reflection on our faith that so much piety should be humdrum, and deadly dull! Private prayer, when it is real action, is the greatest forge of personality. It places a man in direct and effective contact with God the Creator, the source of originality, and especially with God the Redeemer as the source of the new creation. For the minister personality is everything--not geniality, as it is the day's fashion to say, but personality; and prayer is the spring of personality. This impressive personality, due to prayer, you may often have in "the peasant saint." And in some cases its absence is as palpable. Hence comes vulgarity in prayer, essential vulgarity underlying much possible fineness of phrase or manner. Vulgarity in prayer lies not so much in its offenses to good taste in style as in its indications of the absence of spiritual habit and reality. If the theology of rhetoric destroys the theology of reality in the sermon, how much more in prayer!

Prayer is for the religious life what original research is for science--by it we get direct contact with reality. The soul is brought into union with its own vaster nature--God. Therefore, also, we must use the Bible as an original; for indeed, the Bible is the most copious spring of prayer, and of power, and of range. If we learn to pray from the Bible, and avoid a mere cento of its phrases, we shall cultivate in our prayer the large humane note of a universal gospel. Let us nurse our prayer on our study of our Bible; and let us, therefore, not be too afraid of theological prayer. True Christian prayer must have theology in it; no less than true theology must have prayer in it and must be capable of being prayed. "Your theology is too difficult," said Charles V to the Reformers; "it cannot be understood without much prayer." Yes, that is our arduous puritan way. Prayer and theology must interpenetrate to keep each other great, and wide, and mighty. The failure of the habit of prayer is at the root of much of our light distaste for theology. There is a conspiracy of influences round us whose effect is to belittle our great work. Earnest ministers suffer more from the smallness of their people than from their sins, and far more than from their unkindness. Our public may kill by its triviality a soul which could easily resist the assaults of opposition or wickedness. And our newspapers will greatly aid their work. Now, to resist this it is not enough to have recourse to prayer and to cultivate devotion. Unfortunately, there are signs in the religious world to show that prayer and piety alone do not save men from pettiness of interest, thinness of soul, spiritual volatility, the note of insincerity, or foolishness of judgment, or even vindictiveness. The remedy is not prayer alone, but prayer on the scale of the whole gospel and at the depth of searching faith. It is considered prayer--prayer which rises above the childish petitions that disfigure much of our public pietism, prayer which issues from the central affairs of the kingdom of God. It is prayer with the profound Bible as its book of devotion, and a true theology of faith for half of its power. It is the prayer of a mind that moves in Bible passion, and ranges with Bible scope, even when it eschews Bible speech and "the language of Canaan."

And yet, with all its range, it is prayer with concentration. It has not only thought but will in it. The great reason why so many will not decide for Christ is that Christ requires from the world concentration; not seclusion and not renunciation merely, but concentration. And we ministers have our special form of that need. I am speaking not of our share in the common troubles of life, but of those specially that arise from the ministerial office and care. No minister can live up to his work on the casual or interjectional kind of prayer that might be sufficient for many of his flock. He must think, of course, in his prayers--in his private prayers--and he must pray his faith's thought. But, still more, in his praying he must act. Prayer is not a frame of mind, but a great energy. He must rise to conceive his work as an active function of the work of Christ; and he must link his faith, therefore, with the intercession which covers the whole energy of Christ in His kingdom. In this, as in many ways, he must remember, to his great relief and comfort, that it is not he who is the real pastor of his church, but Christ, and that he is but Christ's curate. The final responsibility is not his, but Christ's, who bears the responsibility of all the sins and frets, both of the world and, especially, of the Church.

The concentration, moreover, should correspond to the positivity of the gospel and the Bible. Prayer should rise more out of God's Word and concern for His kingdom than even out of our personal needs, trials, or desires. That is implied in prayer in Christ's name or for Christ's sake, prayer from His place in the midst of the Kingdom. Our Prayer-book, the Bible, does not prescribe prayer, but it does more--it inspires it. And prayer in Christ's name is prayer inspired by His first interest--the gospel. Do not use Christ simply to countersign your egoist petition by a closing formula, but to create, inspire, and glorify it. Prayer in Christ's name is prayer for Christ's object--for His Kingdom, and His promise of the Holy Ghost.

It we really pray for that and yet do not feel we receive it, probably enough we have it; and we are looking for some special form of it not ours, or not ours yet. We may be mistaking the fruits of the Spirit for His presence. Fruits come late. They are different from signs. Buds are signs, and so are other things hard to see. It is the Spirit that keeps us praying for the Spirit, as it is grace that keeps us in grace. Remember the patience of the missionaries who waited in the Spirit fifteen years for their first convert. If God gave His Son unasked, how much more will He give His Holy Spirit to them that ask it! But let us not prescribe the form in which He comes.

The true close of prayer is when the utterance expires in its own spiritual fullness. That is the true Amen. Such times there are. We feel we are at last laid open to God. We feel as though we "did see heaven opened, and the holy angels, and the great God Himself."§ The prayer ends itself; we do not end it. It mounts to its heaven and renders its spirit up to God, saying, "It is finished." It has its perfect consummation and bliss, its spiritually natural close and fruitation, whether it has answer or not.

CHAPTER VII

The Insistency of Prayer

In all I have said I have implied that prayer should be
strenuously importunate. Observe, not petitionary merely,
nor concentrated, nor active alone, but importunate. For
prayer is not only meditation or communion. Nor ought it
to be merely submissive in tone, as the "quietist" ideal is.
We need not begin with "Thy will be done" if we but end
with it. Remember the stress that Christ laid on
importunity. Strenuous prayer will help us to recover the
masculine type of religion--and then our opponents will at
least respect us.

   I would speak a little more fully on this matter of
importunity. It is very closely bound up with the reality
both of prayer and of religion. Prayer is not really a power
till it is importunate. And it cannot be importunate unless it
is felt to have a real effect on the Will of God. I may slip in
here my conviction that far less of the disbelief in prayer is
due to a scientific view of nature's uniformity than to the
slipshod kind of prayer that men hear from us in public
worship; it is often but journalese sent heavenwards, or
phrase-making to carry on. And I would further say that by
importunity something else is meant than passionate
dictation and stormy pertinacity--imposing our egoist will
on God, and treating Him as a mysterious but
manageable power that we may coerce and exploit.

   The deepening of the spiritual life is a subject that

frequently occupies the attention of religious conferences and of the soul bent on self-improvement. But it is not certain that the great saints would always recognize the ideal of some who are addicted to the use of the phrase. The "deepening of the spiritual life" they would find associated with three unhappy things.

1. They would recoil from a use of Scripture prevalent to those circles, which is atomistic individualist, subjective, and fantastic.

2. And what they would feel most foreign to their own objective and penetrating minds might be the air of introspection and self-measurement too often associated with the spiritual thus "deepened"--a spiritual egoism.

3. And they would miss the note of judgment and Redemption.

We should distinguish at the outset *the deepening of spiritual life* from the *quickening of spiritual sensibility.* Christ on the cross was surely deepened in spiritual experience, but was not the essence of that dereliction, and the concomitant of that deepening, the dulling of spiritual sensibility?

There are many plain obstacles to the deepening of spiritual life, amid which I desire to name here only one; it is prayer conceived merely, or chiefly, as submission, resignation, quietism. We say too soon, "Thy will be done"; and too ready acceptance of a situation as His will often means feebleness or sloth. It may be His will that we surmount His will. It may be His higher will that we resist His lower. Prayer is an act of will much more than of sentiment, and its triumph is more than acquiescence. Let us submit when we must, but let us keep the submission in reserve rather than in action, as a ground tone rather than the stole effort. Prayer with us has largely ceased to be wrestling. But is that not the dominant scriptural idea? It is not the sole idea, but is it not the dominant? And is not our subdued note often but superinduced and unreal?

I venture to enlarge on this last head, by way of meeting some who hesitate to speak of the power of prayer to alter God's will. I offer two points:

I. Prayer may really change the will of God, or, if not His will, His intention.

II. It may, like other human energies of godly sort, take the form of resisting the will of God. Resisting His will may be doing His will.

I. As to the first point. If this is not believed the earnestness goes out of prayer. It becomes either a ritual, or a soliloquy only overheard by God; just as thought with the will out of it degenerates into dreaming or brooding, where we are more passive than active. Prayer is not merely the meeting of two moods or two affections, the laying of the head on a divine bosom in trust and surrender. That may have its place in religion, but it is not the nerve and soul of prayer. Nor is it religious reverie. Prayer is an encounter of wills--till one will or the other give way. It is not a spiritual exercise merely, but in its maturity it is a cause acting on the course of God's world.[z] It is, indeed, by God's grace that prayer is a real cause, but such it is. And of course there must be in us a faith corresponding to the grace. Of course also there is always, behind all, the readiness to accept God's will without a murmur when it is perfectly evident and final. "My grace is sufficient for thee." Yes, but there is also the repeated effort to alter its form according to our sanctified needs and desires. You will notice that in Paul's case the power to accept the sufficiency of God's grace only came in the course of an importunate prayer aiming to turn God's hand. Paul ended, rather than began, with "Thy will be done." The peace of God is an end and not a beginning.

"Thy will be done" was no utterance of mere resignation; thought it has mostly come to mean this in a Christianity which tends to canonize the weak instead of strengthening them. As prayer it was a piece of active cooperation with God's will. It was a positive part of it. It is one thing to submit to a stronger will, it is another to be one with it. We submit because we cannot resist it; but when we are one with it we cannot succumb. It is not a power, but our power. But the natural will is not one with God's; and so we come to use these words in a mere negative way, meaning that we cease to resist. Our will does not accept God's, it just stops work. We give in and lie down. But is that the sense of the words in the Lord's Prayer? Do they mean that we have no objection to God's will being done? or that we do not withstand any more? or even that we accept it gladly? Do they not mean something far more positive--that we actively will God's will and aid it, that it is the whole content of our own, that we put into it all the will that there can be in prayer, which is at last the great will power of the race? It is our heart's passion that God's will be done and His kingdom come. And can His kingdom come otherwise than as it is a passion with us? Can His will be done? God's will was not Christ's consent merely, nor His pleasure, but His meat and drink, the source of His energy and the substance of His work.

Observe, nothing can alter God's grace, His will in that sense, His large will and final purpose--our racial blessing, our salvation, our redemption in Jesus Christ. But for that will He is an infinite opportunist. His ways are very flexible. His intentions are amenable to us if His will is changeless. The steps of His process are variable according to our freedom and His.

We are living, let us say, in a careless way; and God proposes a certain treatment of us according to our carelessness. But in the exercise of our spiritual freedom we are by some means brought to pray. We cease to be careless. We pray God to visit us as those who hear. Then He does another thing. He acts differently, with a change caused by our freedom and our change. The treatment for deafness is altered. God adopts another treatment--perhaps for weakness. We have by prayer changed His action, and, so far, His will (at any rate His intention) concerning us. As we pray, the discipline for the prayerless is altered to that for the prayerful. We attain the thing God did not mean to give us unless He had been affected by our prayer. We change the conduct, if not the will, of God to us, the *Verhalten* if not the *Verhaltniss*.

Again, we pray and pray, and no answer comes. The boon does not arrive. Why? Perhaps we are not spiritually ready for it. It would not be a real blessing. But the persistence, the importunity of faith, is having a great effect on our spiritual nature. It ripens. A time comes when we are ready for answer. We then present ourselves to God in a spiritual condition which reasonably causes His to yield. The new spiritual state is not the answer to our prayer, but it is its effect; and it is the condition which makes the answer possible. It makes the prayer effectual. The gift can be a blessing now. So God resists us no more. Importunity prevails, not as mere importunity (for God is not bored into answer), but as the importunity of God's own elect, i.e. as obedience, as a force of the Kingdom, as increased spiritual power, as real moral action, bringing corresponding strength and fitness to receive. I have often found that what I sought most I did not get at the right time, not till it was too late, not till I had learned to do without it, till I had renounced it in principle (though not in desire). Perhaps it had lost some of its zest by the time it came, but it meant more as a gift and a trust. That was God's right time--when I could have it as though I had it not. If it came, it came not to gratify me, but to glorify Him and be a means of serving Him.

One recalls here that most pregnant saying of Schopenhauer: "All is illusion--the hope or the thing hoped." If it is not true for all it is true for very many. Either the hope is never fulfilled or else its fulfilment disappoints. God gives the hoped for thing, but sends leanness into the soul. The mother prays to have a son--and he breaks her heart, and were better dead. Hope may lie to us, or the thing hoped may dash us. But though He slay me I will trust. God does not fail. Amid the wreck of my little world He is firm, and I in Him. I justify God in the ruins; in His good time I shall arrive. More even than my hopes may go wrong. I may go wrong. But my Redeemer liveth; and, great though God is as my Fulfiller, He is greater as my Redeemer. He is great as my hope, but He is greater as my power. What is the failure of my hope from Him compared with the failure of His hope in me? If He continue to believe in me I may well believe in Him.

God's object with us is not to give just so many things and withhold so many; it is to place us in the tissue of His kingdom. His best answer to us is to raise us to the power of answering Him. The reason why He does not answer our prayer is because we do not answer Him and His prayer. And His prayer was, as though Christ did beseech us, "Be ye reconciled." He would lift us to confident business with Him, to commerce of loving wills. The painter wrestles with the sitter till he gives him back himself, and there is a speaking likeness. So man with God, till God surrender His secret. He gives or refuses things, therefore, with a view to that communion alone, and on the whole. It is that spiritual personal end, and not an iron necessity, that rules His course. Is there not a constant spiritual interaction between God and man as free spiritual beings? How that can be is one of the great philosophic problems. But the fact that it is is of the essence of faith. It is the unity of our universe. Many systems try to explain how human freedom and human action are consistent with God's omnipotence and omniscience. None succeed. How secondary causes like man are compatible with God as the Universal and Ultimate Cause is not rationally plain. But there is no practical doubt that they are compatable. And so it is with the action of man on God in prayer. We may perhaps, for the present, put it thus, that we cannot change the will of God, which is grace, and which even Christ never changed but only revealed or effected; but we can change the intention of God, which is a manner of treatment, in the interest of grace, according to the situation of the hour.

If we are guided by the Bible we have much ground for this view of prayer. *Does not Christ set more value upon importunity than on submission?* "Knock, and it shall be opened." I would refer also not only to the parable of the unjust judge, but to the incident of the Syrophenician woman, where her wit, faith, and importunity together did actually change our Lord's intention and break His custom. There there is Paul beseeching the Lord thrice for a boon; and urging us to be instant, insistent, continual in prayer. We have Jacob wrestling. We have Abraham pleading, yea, haggling, with God for Sodom. We have Moses interceding for Israel and asking God to blot his name out of the book of life, if that were needful to save Israel. We have Job facing God, withstanding Him, almost bearding Him, and extracting revelation. And we have Christ's own struggle with the Father in Gethsemane.

It is a wrestle on the greatest scale--all manhood taxed as in some great war, or some great negotiation of State. And the effect is exhaustion often. No, the result of true, prayer is not always peace.

II. As to the second point. This wrestle is in a certain sense a resisting of God. You cannot have wrestling otherwise; but you may have Christian fatalism. It is not mere wrestling with ourselves, our ignorance, our self-will. That is not prayer, but self-torment. Prayer is wrestling with God. And it is better to fall thus into the hands of God than of man--even than our own. It is a resistance that God loves. It is quite foreign to the godless, self-willed defiant resistance. In love there is a kind of resistance that enhances it. The resistance of love is a quite different thing from the resistance of hostility. The yielding to one you love is very different from capitulating to an enemy:

> Two constant lovers, being joined in one,
> Yielding unto each other yield to none -

i.e. to no foreign force, no force foreign to the love which makes them one.

So when God yields to prayer in the name of Christ, to the prayer of faith and love, He yields to Himself who inspired it, as He sware by Himself since none was greater. Christian prayer is the Spirit praying in us. It is prayer in the solidarity of the Kingdom. It is a continuation of Christ's prayer, which in Gethsemane was a wrestle, an sgwnia with the Father. But if so, it is God pleading with God, God dealing with God--as the true atonement must be. And when God yields it is not to an outside influence He yields, but to Himself.

Let me make it still more plain. When we resist the will of God we may be resisting what God wills to be temporary and to be resisted, what He wills to be intermediary and transcended. We resist because God wills we should. We are not limiting God's will, any more than our moral freedom limits it. That freedom is the image of His, and, in a sense, part of His. We should defraud Him and His freedom if we did not exercise ours. So the prayer which resists His dealing may be part of His will and its fulfilment.

Does God not will the existence of things for us to resist, to grapple with? Do we ourselves not appoint problems and make difficulties for those we teach, for the very purpose of their overcoming them? We set questions to children of which we know the answer quite well. The real answer to our will and purpose is not the solution but the grappling, the wrestling. And we may properly give a reward not for the correct answer, but for the hard and honest effort. That work is the prayer; and it has its reward apart from the solution.

That is a principle of education with us. So it may be with God. But I mean a good deal more by this than what is called the reflex action of prayer. It that were all it would introduce an unreality into prayer. We should be praying for exercise, not for action. It would be prayer with a theological form, which yet expects no more than a psychological effect. It would be a prayer which is not sure that God is really more interested in us than we are in Him. But I mean that God's education has a lower stage for us and a higher. He has a lower will and a higher, a prior and a posterior. And the purpose of the lower will is that it be resisted and struggled through to the higher. By God's will (let us say) you are born in a home where your father's earnings are a few shillings a week, like many an English labourer. Is it God's will that you acquiesce in that and never strive out of it? It is God's will that you are there. Is it God's will that you should not resist being there? Nay, it may be His will that you should wisely resist it, and surmount His lower, His initial, will, which is there for the purpose. That is to say, it is His will that you resist, antagonize, His will. And so it is with the state of childhood altogether.

Again: Is disease God's will? We all believe it often is--even if man is to blame for it. It may be, by God's will, the penalty on human ignorance, negligence, or sin. But let us suppose there were only a few cases where disease is God's will. It was so in the lower creatures, before man lived, blundered, or sinned. Take only one such case. Is it God's will that we should lie down and let the disease have its way? Why, a whole profession exists to say no. Medicine exists as an antagonism to disease, even when you can say that disease is God's will and His punishment of sin. A doctor will tell you that resignation is one of his foes. He begins to grow hopeless if the patient is so resigned from the outset as to make no effort, if there be no will to live. Resistance to this ordinance of God's is the doctor's business and the doctor's ally. And why? Because God ordained disease for the purpose of being resisted; He ordained the resistance, that from the conflict man might come out the stronger, and more full of resource and dominion over nature.

Again, take death. It is God's will. It is in the very structure of man, in the divine economy. It is not the result of sin; it was there before sin. Is it to be accepted without demur? Are doctors impious who resist it? Are we sinning when we shrink from it? Does not the life of most people consist in the effort to escape it, in the struggle for a living? So also when we pray and wrestle for another's life, for our dear one's life. "Sir, come down ere my child die." The man was impatient. How familiar we are with his kind! "Do, please, leave your religious talk, which I don't understand; get doing something; cure my child." But was that an impious prayer? It was ignorant, practical, British, but not quite faithless. And it was answered, as many a similar prayer has been. But, then, if death be God's will, to resist it is to resist God's will. Well, it is His will that we should. Christ, who always did God's will, resisted His own death, slipped away from it often, till the hour came; and even then He prayed with all his might against it when it seemed inevitable. "If it be possible, release Me." He was ready to accept it, but only in the last resort, only if there was no other way, only after every other means had been exhausted. To the end He cherished the fading hope that there might be some other way. He went to death voluntarily, freely, but--shall we say reluctantly?-- resisting the most blessed act of God's will that ever was performed in heaven or on earth; resisting, yet sure to acquiesce when that was God's clear will.

The whole nature, indeed, is the will of God, and the whole of grace is striving with nature. It is our nature to have certain passions. That is God's will. But it is our calling of God to resist them as much as to gratify them. There are there as God's will to be resisted as much as indulged. The redemption from the natural man includes the resistance to it, and the release of the soul from what God Himself appointed as its lower stages--never as its dwelling place, and never its tomb. So far prayer is on the lines of evolution.

Obedience is the chief end. But obedience is not mere submission, mere resignation. It is not always acquiescence, even in prayer. We obey God as much when we urge our suit, and make a real petition of it, as when we accept His decision; as much when we try to change His will as when we bow to it. The kingdom of heaven suffereth violence. There is a very fine passage in Dante, Parad. xx. 94 (Longfellow):

> Regnum coelorum suffereth violence
> From fervent love, and from that living hope
> That overcometh the divine volition.
> Not in the way that man o'ercometh man;
> We conquer it because it will be conquered,
> And, conquered, conquers by benignity.

It is His will--His will of grace--that prayer should prevail with Him and extract blessings. And how we love the grace that so concedes them! The answer to prayer is not the complaisance of a playful power lightly yielding to the playful egoism of His favorites. "Our antagonist is our helper." To struggle with Him is one way of doing His will. To resist is one way of saying, "Thy will be done." It was God's will that Christ should deprecate the death God required. It pleased God as much as His submission to death. But could it have been pleasing to Him that Christ should pray so, if no prayer could ever possibly change God's will? Could Christ have prayed so in that belief? Would faith ever inspire us to pray if the God of our faith must be unmoved by prayers? The prayer that goes to an inflexible God, however good He is, is prayer that rises more from human need than from God's own revelation, or from Christian faith (where Christian prayer should rise). It is His will, then, that we should pray against what seems His will, and what, for the lower stage of our growth, is His will. And all this without any unreality whatever.

Let us beware of a pietist fatalism which thins the spiritual life, saps the vigour of character, makes humility mere acquiescence, and piety only feminine, by banishing the will from prayer as much as thought has been banished from it. "The curse of so much religion" (I have quoted Meredith) "is that men cling to God with their weakness rather than with their strength."

The popularity of much acquiescence is not because it is holier, but because it is easier. And an easy gospel is the consumption that attacks Christianity. It is the phthisis to faith.

Once come to think that we best say "Thy will be done" when we acquiesce, when we resign, and not also when we struggle and wrestle, and in time all effort will seem less pious than submission. And so we fall into the ecclesiastical type of religion, drawn from an age whose first virtue was submission to outward superiors. We shall come to canonize decorum and subduedness in life and worship (as the Episcopal Church with its monarchical ideas of religion has done). We shall think more of order than of effort, more of law than of life, more of fashion than of faith, of good form than of great power. But was subduedness the mark of the New Testament men? Our religion may gain some beauty in this way, but it loses vigour. It may gain style, but it loses power. It is good form, but mere aesthetic piety. It may consecrate manners, but it improverishes the mind. It may regulate prayer by the precepts of intelligence instead of the needs and faith of the soul. It may feed certain pensive emotions, but it may emasculate will, secularize energy, and empty character. And so we decline to a state of things in which we have no shocking sins--yes, and no splendid souls; when all souls are dully correct, as like as shillings, but as thin, and as cheap.

All our forms and views of religion have their test in prayer. Lose the importunity of prayer, reduce it to soliloquy, or even to colloquy, with God, lose the real conflict of will and will, lose the habit of wrestling and the hope of prevailing with God, make it mere walking with God in friendly talk; and, precious as that is, yet you tend to lose the reality of prayer at last. In principle you make it mere conversation instead of the soul's great action. You lose the food of character, the renewal of will. You may have beautiful prayers--but as ineffectual as beauty so often is, and as fleeting. And so in the end you lose the reality of religion. Redemption turns down into mere revelation, faith to assent, and devotion to a phase of culture. For you lose the power of the Cross and so of the soul.

Resist God, in the sense of rejecting God, and you will not be able to resist any evil. But resist God in the sense of closing with God, cling to Him with your strength, not your weakness only, with your active and not only your passive faith, and He will give you strength. Cast yourself into His arms not to be caressed but to wrestle with Him. He loves that holy war. He may be too many for you, and lift you from your feet. But it will be to lift you from earth, and set you in the heavenly places which are their who fight the good fight and lay hold of God as their eternal life.

16211529R00070

Printed in Great Britain
by Amazon